T0198913

THE POWER *of* VOICE

A Supernatural Gift From God

Emmanuel Kwame Bempong

Order this book online at www.trafford.com
or email orders@trafford.com

Most Trafford titles are also available at major online book retailers.

Printed in the United States of America.

ISBN: 978-1-4669-0375-3 (sc)
ISBN: 978-1-4669-0381-4 (e)

Trafford rev. 06/16/2012

 www.trafford.com

North America & international
toll-free: 1 888 232 4444 (USA & Canada)
phone: 250 383 6864 ♦ fax: 812 355 4082

Contents

A gift opens the way for the giver and ushers him into the presence of the great.

(*Proverbs 18:16*)

About the Book

This revelation has been sought for centuries but has finally been revealed. The supernatural God-given talent (gift) to all mankind is the power of *voice*.

The concept of this book is inspirational, motivational, revelation knowledge from the Holy Spirit, which reveals the divine supernatural gift God Almighty deposited in mankind (human beings) when he formed and created us.

This exposes us to the effectiveness, the power, the blessings, and the benefits of our *voices*. Many believe God placed on mankind our possessions, inheritance, and blessings before we were born, but the question is: what reveals or makes it possible for the blessings within us to come out so we can see and enjoy them?

"A gift opens the way for the giver and ushers him into the presence of the great"

(Proverbs 18:16).

Our voice, Children of God, is a supernatural gift in us we need to value and motivate to function properly.

Dedication

This book is dedicated to my lord, master, and savior Jesus Christ and the entire host in heaven and also to my loved ones, those whom I know and those I don't.

And most of all, I dedicate this book to my friends out there who have the desire to do something with their lives but whom failure and the irresponsible spirit of timidity are keeping in captivity.

May the powerful and divine impartation on this book be released unto them. May it cause them to come out of themselves to do something with their talents through their voices so that they may see prosperity, success, and riches, because there might be many souls out there who are dependent on their progress to survive.

God bless you.

Foreword

The *Power of Voice* warrants our attention and summons our senses to the realization that every individual is what he or she says! Your world is created by your own word! This piece of heavenly information gradually points out how to activate the strength, magnitude, and intensity of your voice to cause a change in the world we live in; I mean both the spiritual and physical world. Mind you, it's always the devil's duty to cause you to zip your lips.

The author carefully downloads from the Throne Room of Heaven how to recognize and use your God-given talent (gift). I know everybody is created with a special gift or talent, but only a few have noticed and are fully operating with it to affect mankind.

In my many years of ministry, I've come across people who carry gifts, but most of them are dormant, inactive, static, and nonoperational just because these people don't know how to activate them. I've known the author for some time and have seen him moved from grace to grace, because he has been able to use the power and the strength of his voice to make his world dynamic. I strongly recommend this book to everyone, and I can guarantee that your life will be transformed for the better.

Prophet Daniel Amoateng

Founder / General Overseer of Power of Worship International and President of Power Outreach Worldwide

Acknowledgments

My deepest and greatest gratitude is for my wonderful sweetheart, Casandra Y. Appiah, for accompanying me on this journey.

She stands behind me and supports and encourages me; she also edited and directed the grammar of this book.

Woman of God, may you be filled with everlasting joy all the days of your life and may everlasting salvation be your crown.

I also give a sacrificial thankfulness to the E-Save Group of Companies.

Summary

This Revelation has been sought for centuries but finally been revealed through my new book—titled: **THE POWER OF VOICE**—a supernatural gift from God.

Brothers and Sisters I only need you to take a few minutes to think about your voice and you will know that without it you wouldn't have been where you are. And if you have voice and you are not blessed then I urge you to activate and motivate it to be a blessing and a benefit in this world. Voice can not be seen, feel or touched yet it can be described as something visible and this makes it supernatural.

Friends, I need you to notice this "*have you ever seen or heard any deaf, mute & dump person, a superstar, celebrity, men or women of God in the world*". Even if you have, are they famous or successful like those having a voice?

People of God, I take this opportunity to proclaim to you that your voice is a supernatural God given gift He placed in you. Therefore it is only your voice that can activate and motivate the gifts or talents in you and lead you be a blessing to the four corners of the earth.

In This Book titled: **THE POWER OF VOICE**—a Supernatural Gift from God reveals to us;

- It was the supernatural voice behind the word of God that brought creation into existence. Imagine if voice is not necessary or supernatural as I am proclaiming, God would have wrote some words in the air or some where in the clouds for the Universe to come into existence.

- Many marriages have suffered divorce and relationships are suffering from separation because both partners are lacking to use their voice appropriately towards each other due to lack of humbleness in their voices.

- Friends think about the Superstars, Celebrities, men and women of God around you, supposing they had no voice would they have been where they are or who they are. Coming to think of it is even your praising voice and elevating voices that is making them famous and successful.

- Also in this Book reveals the powerful tool of Lucifer (SATAN) which is his Voice—People of God, the devil does not put pressure or Force mankind to involve him or her into doing wrong but with his voice leads us into destruction. With the Devils Voice convince Adam and Eve to break the loyalty between mankind and God. Friends it only took the powerful Voice of Lucifer to convince even Holy Angels in Heaven to join him in war against God. This tells us that the powerful tool of SATAN is his Voice.

Friends, Each and every single soul, life, believer or unbeliever that exists on this earth can read this book; is inspirational, revelational and motivational.

Introduction

This book, *The Power of Voice*, is inspirational and contains deep revelation knowledge from the Holy Spirit, which divinely reveals to us who we really are and the perfect supernatural gift God Almighty deposited in mankind after he created and formed us.

As a strong Christian growing up, I heard preaching (sermons) that made me believe so strongly that God Almighty, the Creator of Heaven and Earth, has placed in mankind *riches*, *blessings*, *possessions*, and *inheritance*.

By this, I mean the good things in mankind he placed in us when he created and formed us. And all we need to do as his believers is make them come out of us and enjoy them. I believe as a Christian that, one way or another, God our Creator has given to each and every single person on earth his or her gift (talent) to manifest it.

And the Word of God confirms this:

> There are different kinds of gifts, but the same spirit. There are different kinds of services, but the same Lord. There are different kinds of working, but the same God works all of them in all men.

Now to each one the manifestation of the spirit is given for the common good. To one there is given through the spirit the message of wisdom, to another the gift of healing by that one spirit, to another miraculous powers, to another prophesy, to another distinguishing between spirits, to another speaking in different kinds of tongues, and to still another, the interpretation of tongues. All these are the work of one and the same spirit, and he gives them to each one, just as he determines. (1 Corinthians 12:4-11)

This is about spiritual gifts given by the Spirit of God, which God deposited in mankind after his creation. The Bible also gives us a perfect story in the parable of the God-given talent which Jesus told his disciples:

Again, it will be like a man going on a journey, which called his servants and entrusted his property to them. To one he gave five talents of money, to another two talents, and to another one talent, each according to his ability. Then he went on his journey.

The man who had received the five talents went at once and put his money to work and gained five more. So also, the one with the two talents gained two more. But the man who had received one talent went off, dug a hole in the ground and hid his master's money.

After a long time the master of those servants returned and settled accounts with them. The man who had received the five talents brought the other five. "Master," he said, "you entrusted me with five talents. See, I have gained five more."

His master replied, "Well done, good and faithful servant! You have been faithful with a few things; I will put you in charge of many things. Come and share your master's happiness!"

The man with two talents also came. "Master," he said, "you entrusted me with two talents; see, I have gained two more."

His master replied, "Well done, good and faithful servant! You have been faithful with a few things; I will put you in charge of many things. Come and share your master's happiness!"

Then the man who had received the one talent came. "Master," he said, "I knew that you are a hard man, harvesting where you have not sown and gathering where you have not scattered seed. So I was afraid and went out and hid your talent in the ground. See, here is what belongs to you."

His master replied, "You wicked, lazy servant! So you knew that I harvested where I have not sown and gather where I have not scattered seed? Well then, you should have put my money on deposit with the bankers, so that when I returned I would have received it back with interest. Take the talent from him and give it to the one who has the ten talents. For everyone who has will be given more, and he will have an abundance. Whoever does not have, even what he has will be taken from him. And throw that worthless servant outside, into the darkness, where there will be weeping and gnashing of teeth." (Matthew 25:14-30)

In the above story (parable), we are made to realize that there will be a curse on mankind if we refuse to operate, activate, and manifest our talents God Almighty has given to us, and it will lead to mankind's destruction. But what I keep on asking myself and the Holy Spirit is: what is the key to open or operate these talents (gifts), and how will I or other children of God be able to make these sweet things in me be available and enjoy them?

Suddenly, the word *prayer* came to my thoughts, but I believe Christians already know prayer is our access as believers to make manifest in the physical and spiritual world. Then I asked the Holy Spirit again, as a mature Christian. At my level, I sometimes realize or witness and testify that it's not every Christian or believer whose prayers are answered or if answered, the responses seem to take forever.

I also see Christians who often complain about how they are suffering from rejections and sometimes even feel that situations make them unaware of their involvement in the Christian world, though they pray, fast, read the Bible, and go to church as well. Immediately, the Holy Spirit whispered in my ears, "It is because their voice can't be recognized; their voice can't be identified; their voice doesn't gain favor (in other words, their voice is not pleasing) in the sight of God."

Why? Because there is no humility in their voice;

"For God opposes the proud but gives grace to the humble" (James 4:6)).

Their voice! Their voice!

Whose voice? Their voice!

Our voice! Your voice, how interesting . . .

So, Children of God, all the while, our voice has been the key (access) to activating, operating, and manipulating our gifts (talents), which have been deposited in us by God, so that they will come out of us and we can enjoy them. If only we knew how to present and preserve it before God.

If you remember, the voice of the Lord brought creation into existence, as you read in the book of Genesis from the Bible:

> And God said, "Let there be light," and there was light. God saw the light was good, and he separated the light from the darkness. God called the light "day," and the darkness he called "night." And there was evening, and there was morning—the first day. And God said, "Let there be an expanse between the waters to separate water from water." So God made the expanse and separated the water under the expanse from the water above it. And it was so. God called the expanse "sky." And there was evening, and there was morning—the second day.
>
> And God said, "Let the water under the sky be gathered to one place, and let dry ground appear." And it was so. God called the dry ground "land," and the gathered waters

he called "seas." And God saw that it was good. Then God said, "Let the land produce vegetation: seed-bearing plants and trees on the land that bear fruit with seed in it, according to their various kinds."

And it was so. The land produced vegetation: plants bearing seed according to their kinds and trees bearing fruit with seed in it according to their kinds. And God saw that it was good. And there was evening, and there was morning—the third day. And God said, "Let there be lights in the expanse of the sky to separate the day from the night, and let them serve as signs to mark seasons and days and years, and let them be lights in the expanse of the sky to give light on the earth."

And it was so. God made two great lights—the greater light to govern the day and the lesser light to govern the night. He also made the stars. God set them in the expanse of the sky to give light on the earth, to govern the day and the night, and to separate light from darkness. And God saw that it was good. And there was evening and there was morning—the fourth day. And God said, "Let the water teem with living creatures, and let birds fly above the earth across the expanse of the sky."

So God created the great creatures of the sea and every living and moving thing with which the water teems, according to their kinds, and every winged bird according to its kind. And God saw that it was good. God blessed them and said, "Be fruitful and increase in number and fill the water in the seas, and let the birds increase on the earth."

And there was evening, and there was morning—the fifth day. And God said, "Let the land produce living creatures according to their kinds: livestock, creatures that move along the ground, and wild animals, according to their kinds, and all the creatures that move along the ground according to their kinds."

And God saw that it was good. Then God said, "Let us make man in our image, in our likeness, and let them rule over the fish of the sea and the birds of the air, over the fish of the sea and the birds of the air, over the livestock, over all the earth, and over all the creatures that move along the ground." (Genesis 1:3-26)

The above scriptures are very powerful and more interesting if you will study them carefully and gain the insight. We notice that God was speaking as well as talking and the universe was coming into being. Believers, this is wonderful, but with my insight, I noticed that it is not just the words; there is a supernatural force behind his words, which is his *voice*.

First of all, believers, what even makes the words of the Lord come out for hearing? Don't you think it is the voice that makes words be heard? I need you to picture this carefully, because it is very deep revelation knowledge; if it's just words and not his voice, then the Lord could have just written some words in the heavens or anywhere in the clouds, and everything would have come into existence.

But we realize that that wasn't the process. His voice was the sound that came out with His words to bring forth creation.

Therefore, I would define voice as the sweet or ugly sound that comes out with our words. It is also the sound that cometh with our words for our words to be heard. Believers, this is because the tone or sound of a word can make it ugly, but with a different tone or sound, that word can be sweet.

I want to set you thinking at this point: do you think you could just write a few words of your choice on a sheet of paper or any type of material and show it to a person who is demon-possessed and the demons will come out of that person? No! It is never done that way; you need your voice to shout the devil out of that person because there is power in our *voice*.

Is true believers! Imagine how provoking, annoying, and irritating it is if you are watching a nice movie on your television and the volume (sound) is muted or not functioning. The movie becomes meaningless, though it is said to be nice.

The spirit of the Lord is upon this book, which the Lord will be using as a *supernatural* tool to shape and sharpen people's voices. Many voices of those who read this book will be heard all over the earth and in the heavenly realms. The supernatural revelations in this book will expose salvation to people, and spiritually or physically mute and deaf people will receive their voices to speak. Many dead marriages will be resurrected, and determined Christians are going to be everlastingly rich through the divine activation of their voices.

This book will also reveal to you the insight and outsight of the devil (Satan)—how he is really powerless, but because of his voice, he can cause and lead mankind to destruction as he did with the angels in heaven. With his supernatural voice, he even convinced holy angels to join him and also support him in his evil thoughts against God. With his voice, he also convinced Eve to disobey and break the loyalty between God and mankind in the Garden of Eden.

It was also the *voice* of the Lord that revealed the future to John when he was on the island of Patmos for the book of Revelation.

Chapter One

Identification, Recognition, and Communication

*V*OICES ARE THE sweetest or ugliest sounds that come out with our words. They are also the sound or tones that come with our words so that our words can be heard.

A voice cannot be seen, felt, or touched, yet it can be described, identified, and recognized and serves as a means of communication between people. Voices can be described or identified as beautiful, ugly, nice, sweet, good, unique, humble, feeble, anguished, irritating, provoking, filthy, decent, wonderful, marvelous, powerful, etc. However, we normally see, feel, and touch things that have descriptions matching those mentioned above.

Nonetheless, with *voice*, we cannot see, touch, or feel it, yet it can be described as something visible. This makes it *"supernatural and a powerful gift from God."*

I want to set you thinking: imagine if the world is just as it is but there was no voice to communicate with—to talk, sing, or pray with; how awful and empty the world would still be. So, you see, the world would still be meaningless if not for our voice, though there would still be creatures occupying it. If we will remember, even the world came into existence through the powerful voice of the Most High God.

With the powerful voice of the Lord, He called things that were not, and these things came into existence. Just imagine you speaking (pronouncing) things of your hearts desires by using your voice, and they are all coming into being. How would you feel? It will make you feel so superior, powerful, and overjoyed, which is normally happens to determined and powerful Christians.

> And God said, "Let there be light," and there was light. God saw the light was good, and he separated the light from the darkness. God called the light "day," and the darkness he called "night." And there was evening, and there was morning—the first day. And God said, "Let there be an expanse between the waters to separate water from water." So God made the expanse and separated the water under the expanse from the water above it. And it was so. God called the expanse "sky." And there was evening, and there was morning—the second day.
>
> And God said, "Let the water under the sky be gathered to one place, and let dry ground appear." And it was so. God called the dry ground "land," and the gathered waters he called "seas." And God saw that it was good. Then God said, "Let the land produce vegetation: seed-bearing plants and

trees on the land that bear fruit with seed in it, according to their various kinds." And it was so. The land produced vegetation: plants bearing seed according to their kinds and trees bearing fruit with seed in it according to their kinds. And God saw that it was good.

And there was evening, and there was morning—the third day. And God said, "Let there be lights in the expanse of the sky to separate the day from the night, and let them serve as signs to mark seasons and days and years, and let them be lights in the expanse of the sky to give light on the earth." And it was so. God made two great lights—the greater light to govern the day and the lesser light to govern the night.

He also made the stars. God set them in the expanse of the sky to give light on the earth, to govern the day and the night, and to separate light from darkness. And God saw that it was good.

And there was evening and there was morning—the fourth day. And God said, "Let the water teem with living creatures, and let birds fly above the earth across the expanse of the sky."

So God created the great creatures of the sea and every living and moving thing with which the water teems, according to their kinds, and every winged bird according to its kind. And God saw that it was good.

God blessed them and said, "Be fruitful and increase in number and fill the water in the seas, and let the birds increase on the earth." And there was evening, and there was morning—the fifth day.

And God said, "Let the land produce living creatures according to their kinds: livestock, creatures that move along the ground, and wild animals, according to their kinds, and all the creatures that move along the ground according to their kinds.

And God saw that it was good. Then God said, "Let us make man in our image, in our likeness, and let them rule over the fish of the sea and the birds of the air, over the livestock, over all the earth, and over all the creatures that move along the ground. (Genesis 1:3-26)

Looking at this story, we notice, that with his voice, God called things into existence, and as children of the Most High God, we believe very strongly from the Holy Scriptures that;

In the beginning was the word and the word was with GOD. He was with GOD in the beginning. Through him, all things were made; without him, nothing was made that has been made. (John 1:1-3).

Now this is totally true, but I need you to imagine that there was a supernatural force behind the word of God, which is his *voice*.

And God being so good has given mankind (Creatures) on earth *voices* to operate and manifest our gifts (talents). We need to believe that with our *voices*, we can also talk, sing, pray, and prophesy for things to come into existence. At this point, I can strongly testify by faith that *voice* is a supernatural gift God has given to mankind to be a benefit and a blessing for us in his kingdom on earth and his kingdom in heaven (paradise).

These moments direct my attention to the Lord's creation. After the creation of man, the first thing God commanded man to do was for Adam to use his voice to operate by naming all his living creatures.

> *Now the Lord God had formed out of the ground all the beasts of the field and all the birds of the air. He brought them to the man to see what he would name them; and whatever the man called each living creature, that was its name. So the man gave names to all the livestock, the birds of the air and all the beasts of the field. (Genesis 2:19-20)*

What a privilege we have! With the above story, we realize that mankind has been given the key (access) to operate in his gift, and during this period, there was a process for mankind to activate their communication skills. In other words, God also taught mankind how to talk, pray, prophesy, and call things into existence. What a powerful and supernatural gift!

Let me set you thinking again. Imagine, when a new baby (creature) is born, God never refuses to allow the baby's voice to cry or make noise for his or her parents to know what is wrong.

Believers, isn't this awesome?

By the power of the Holy Spirit, let's set our minds back on the story, before Christ Jesus began his ministry.

> Every year his parents went to Jerusalem for the feast of the Passover. When he was twelve years old, they went up to the feast, according to the custom. After the feast was over, while his parents were returning home, the boy Jesus stayed behind in Jerusalem, but they were unaware of it. Thinking he was in their company, they travelled on for a day.
>
> Then they began looking for him among their relatives and friends. When they did not find him, they went back to Jerusalem to look for him.
>
> After three days they found him in the temple courts, sitting among the teachers, listening to them and asking them questions. Everyone who heard him was amazed at his understanding and his answers. (Luke 2:41-47)

At the tender age of twelve, the first thing he did was exercise his communication skills to operate through his voice, because that was the key for him to pray, preach, prophesy, and perform healings, miracles, and the signs and wonders that he did. So Jesus sneaks into the temple and begins to communicate with the elders and priests of the Law of Moses. And by his sweet voice and good words, he talked so well that all liked him and were amazed.

I hope you are wondering at this moment, and I know the Holy Spirit has given you the insight and outsight of the supernatural gift God Almighty has deposited in you. With your sweet voice and good words, you can make things be as they are supposed to be in the sight of the living God and also stand before kings, queens, presidents, and pastors, etc.

But the Holy Spirit made me aware that it is not just using your voice any how or way; there must be a recognition and identification of your voice in the sight of the Lord God Almighty as the voice of *righteousness* (humility) or *unrighteousness* (pride).

Now remember that the Lord's ear is very attentive to the righteous' prayers:

"The eyes of the LORD are on the righteous and his ears are attentive to their cry" (Psalm 34:15).

But why is the Lord's ear very attentive to the righteous' prayers? Because of our humble voice but the unrighteousness voice come with the voice of pride. I hope you can remember the story (parable) of the Pharisee and the tax collector.

> To some who were confident of their own righteousness and looked down on everybody else, Jesus told this parable: "Two men went up to the temple to pray, one a Pharisee and the other a tax collector. The Pharisee stood up and prayed about himself: 'God, I thank you that I am not like other men—robbers, evildoers, adulterers—or even like this tax collector. I fast twice a week and give a tenth of all I get.' But the tax collector stood at a distance. He would not even look up to heaven, but beat his breast and said, 'God, have mercy on me, a sinner.' I tell you that this man, rather than the other, went home justified before God. For

everyone who exalts himself will be humbled, and he who humbles himself will be exalted." (Luke 18:9-14)

Believers, could you just imagine two Christians at the temple praying, and one is said to be humble in his voice and other is said to be proud. My fellow Christians, why are humbleness and pride so important in our voice? I believe it is because God opposes the proud and gives grace to the humble. Therefore, I urge my brothers and sisters to try as much as possible to let there be humbleness in their voices, so their requests before God can be granted.

Another deep revelation from a story in the Bible will make us aware of how people can identify your *voice* and recognize you by your voice.

> Jacob said to his father, "I am Esau your firstborn. I have done as you told me. Please sit up and eat some of my game so that you may give me your blessing."
>
> Isaac asked his son, "How did you find it so quickly, my son?"
>
> "The Lord your God gave me success," he replied.
>
> Then Isaac said to Jacob, "Come near so I can touch you, my son, to know whether you really are my son Esau or not." Jacob went close to his father Isaac, who touched him and said, "The voice is the voice of Jacob, but the hands are the hands of Esau." (Genesis 27:19-22)

We see it very clearly that our voices are easily recognized by the people who know us; so does God distinguish between voices, and we can never disguise our voice before God.

A similar and very interesting story from the Bible gives us clarity on how someone who knows you very well can identify your *voice*. It doesn't matter how young or old the person is.

"When she recognized Peter's voice, she was so overjoyed she ran back without opening it and exclaimed, 'Peter is at the door!'" (Acts 12:14)

In this verse, the little girl who went to check who was at the door could recognize Peter by his voice without even opening the door for him first. How interesting.

Another insight can also been gained from the Bible in the following passage:

> *"Saul recognized David's voice and said 'Is that your voice, David my son?'*
>
> *"David replied, 'Yes it is, my lord the king.'"* (1 Samuel 26:17)

In the story, King Saul was able to recognize and identify David by his voice. Isn't this marvelous and wonderful, my fellow Christians? God Almighty always recognizes and identifies us by our voices.

And all this while you have a voice and you are refusing to be blessed and also be a blessing to the people around you.

It is my prayer at this point that the Holy Spirit should renew, refresh, restore, and empower your voice and also teach you and give you the insight into how you will be able to operate in your voice.

Amen!

Chapter Two

The Expressing of Voice (The Power of Voice)

$\mathcal{A}$PPARENTLY, VOICES CAN only be distinguished based on how they are expressed. It is with the expression of a person's voice that you can distinguish or determine what he or she means, and it is also by a person's behavior (moments) that you will be able to define the expressions of their voice.

Believers, this is because the tone or sound of a word can make it be ugly while that same word with a different tone or sound can be meant to be sweet. Some words from a person can be meant to be insulting or very harsh, and those same words from the person can be meant to be lovely and good, depending on the voice, tone, or pitch the person uses.

God's living creatures' (mankind's) voices can be categorized and be differentiated in many ways, such as a shouting voice; a speaking voice; a weeping voice; a crying voice; a preaching voice; a praying voice; a praising voice; an angry voice; a complaining voice; a happy voice; etc.

Believers, as we read in the previous chapter, two people went to the temple to pray but with differentiation in their voices: one was known to be humble, and the other was known to be proud.

I would love for you to get references to support the different types of voice mentioned above by following this Biblical chapter and verse.

In the Bible, it says:

"Then some Levites from the kohathites and koranhites stood up and praised the Lord, the God of Israel with a very loud voice" (2 Chronicles 20:19).

"One of them, when he saw he was healed, came back, praising God in a loud voice" (Luke 17:15).

"You, who bring good tidings to Zion, go up on a high mountain. You, who bring good tidings to Jerusalem, lift up your voice with a shout, lift it up, and do not be afraid; say to the towns of Judah, 'Here is your God!'" (Isaiah 40:9).

"Hear me, O God, as I voice my complaint: Protect my life from the threat of the enemy" (Psalm 64:1).

This is what the LORD says: "A voice is heard in Ramah, mourning and great weeping, Rachel weeping for her children and refusing to be comforted, because her children are no more.

This is what the LORD says: "Restrain your voice from weeping and your eyes from tears, for your work will be rewarded," declares the LORD. "They will return from the land of the enemy." (Jeremiah 31:15-16)

As the Bible explains to us, there are different ways of expressing mankind's voice; we can totally understand how important our voices are. And God's living creatures on earth can do nothing without our voice. I want to make it clear that everything under the sun mankind can think of when it comes to God's living creatures needs a voice to *proact*.

Thus, God knew how relevant mankind will need voice to operate and without this *supernatural*, God-given gift, mankind can't do anything. Think about this: with all the activities that go on under the sun, we can reach the conclusion that voice is used to do everything and anything. We use our voices to request favors, pray, preach, sing, talk etc.

And even with the crafts (skillful or creative) men who also use their hands (fingers) to create artifacts, after their work is done, they use their voices to express the means of their performance or you can not be an athelet if you don't have a voice.

You just continue to imagine all the activities in the world with God's living creatures; you will find no activity that doesn't need voice to manifest also since I grew up I have never seen or heard any deaf, mute and dump person a celebrity, superstar, president, musician, preacher or an athelet but even if there are some in the world, they are not as famous or successful than those having a voice

Chapter Three

The Voice of God

*T*HE VOICE OF the Lord is powerful; the voice of the Lord is majestic. The voice of the Lord breaks the cedars; the voice of the Lord strikes with flashes of lightning. The voice of the Lord shakes the desert; the voice of the Lord twists the oaks and strips the forests bare.

From the Bible, we found out how powerful, fearful and proactive the expressing of God's voice is. There is much power in God's voice, which is accompanied by fire, sounds like thunder, and comes forth to accomplish great things.

A story in the Bible made me understood how God's voice can also come in a gentle whisper.

> After the earthquake came a fire, but the Land was not the fire. And after the fire came a gentle whisper. When Elijah heard it, he pulled his cloak over his face and went out and

stood at the mouth of the cave. Then a voice said to him, "What are you doing here, Elijah?" (1 Kings 19:12-13)

Isn't this supernatural?

Also from the Bible are the following words:

"The LORD thundered from heaven; the voice of the Most High resounded" (2 Samuel 22:14).

> After that came the sound of his roar; he thunders with his majestic voice. When his voice resounds, he holds nothing back. God's voice thunders in marvelous ways; he does great things beyond our understanding. (Job 37:4-5).

According to the Bible, the voice of God sounds like thunder and there is much power in his voice.

And again in the Bible, it says:

> The voice of the LORD is over the waters; the God of glory thunders, the LORD thunders over the mighty waters. The voice of the LORD is powerful; the voice of the LORD is majestic. The voice of the LORD breaks the cedars of Lebanon. He makes Lebanon skip like a calf, Sirion like a young wild ox. The voice of the LORD strikes with flashes of lightening. The voice of the LORD shakes the desert; the LORD shakes the Desert of Kadesh. The voice of the LORD twists the oaks and strips the forest bare. And in his temple all cry, "Glory!" (Psalm 29:3-9)

The proactivity of God's voice came forth to accomplish great things.

"Nations are in uproar, kingdoms fall; he lifts his voice, the earth melts" (Psalm 46:6).

Believers, we now understand that anytime God uses His voice, something is fulfilled; the voice of the Lord comes in accomplishment of something. This gives us, as children of God, a clear motivation for our voice; God has given us this because it is meant to accomplish something in our lives.

Therefore, we need to use it wisely, humbly, and righteously according to the directions and the instructions of the Holy Spirit; with them, we will achieve many goals and accomplish His purpose and fulfill our destiny. And as believers of the Most High God, it is very important and necessary for us to recognize our Lord God Almighty's voice, and listen to his voice. We must recognize his voice, as Apostle John made us aware:

> The watchman opens the gate for him, and the sheep listen to his voice. He calls his own sheep by name and leads them out. When he has brought out all his own, he goes on ahead of them, and his sheep follow him because they know his voice. But they will never follow a stranger; in fact, they will run away from him because they do not recognize a stranger's voice. (John 10:3-5)

And we must listen to God's voice:

He said, "If you listen carefully to the voice of the LORD your God and do what is right in his eyes, if you pay attention to his commands and keep all his decrees, I will not bring on you any diseases I brought on the Egyptians, for I am the LORD, who heals you. (Exodus 15:26).

And that you may love the LORD your God, listen to his voice, and hold fast to him. For the LORD is your life, and he will give you many years in the land he swore to give to your fathers, Abraham, Isaac and Jacob. (Deuteronomy 30:20)

Again, we must obey his voice as the Holy Scriptures made us aware:

But Samuel replied: "Does the LORD delight in burnt offerings and sacrifices as much as in obeying the voice of the LORD? To obey is better than sacrifice and to heed is better than the fat of rams. (1 Samuel 15:22)

Then Zerubbabel son of Shealtiel, Joshua son of Jehozadak, the high priest, and the whole remnant of the people obeyed the voice of the LORD their God and the message of the prophet Haggai, because the LORD their God had sent him. And the people feared the LORD. (Haggai 1:12)

My fellow believers, I hope and believe so strongly that up to this very moment as you have been reading this book, you have felt the power of your voice being moved by the deep revelational knowledge of the Holy Spirit. May the Holy Spirit renew, restore, refresh, and empower your voice to invoke the gifting in you so you become a pillar of success.

By the remembrance power of the Holy Spirit, you could remember from the Holy Scriptures that many are *called* but few are *chosen*. This powerful word explains to us that everything you have accomplished or are still accomplishing is by the call of God, which is through *His supernatural voice* He used to call you. It has been an impartation or has placed an impartation in your life.

Because the voice of the Lord came forth to fulfill or accomplish something, so when God calls you, your life becomes a fulfillment; in other words, your life becomes an accomplishment.

And man receives nothing until it has been given to him from heaven above:

"To this John replied, 'A man can receive only what is given to him from heaven'" (John 3:27).

Furthermore, let's refresh our memory on the influential great men of God, called by the *Lord's voice* from the Holy Scriptures:

When the LORD saw that he had gone over to look, God called to him from within the bush, "Moses! Moses!"

And Moses said, "Here I am."

"Do not come any closer," God said. "Take off your sandals, for the place where you are standing is a holy ground." Then he said, "I am the God of your father, the God of

Abraham, the God of Isaac and the God of Jacob." At this, Moses hid his face, because he was afraid to look at God. (Exodus 3:4-6)

Moses, a humble servant and prophet of the Lord, was called by the voice of the Lord, one day while he was attending to his father-in-law's sheep. And when we read through the story, we see that his life became a fulfillment. His purpose on earth became accomplished by the call of God, when he led the Israelites from Egypt throughout the desert to Canaan.

> When he saw this, he was amazed at the sight. As he went over to look more closely, he heard the Lord's voice: "I am the God of your fathers, the God of Abraham, Isaac and Jacob." Moses trembled with fear and did not dare to look. (Acts 7:31-32)

This passage tells about the powerful voice that called Moses from the fire and how the purpose of his destiny came to fulfillment. You know, Brothers and Sisters, at this moment, I want you to value whoever you are, especially if you have the "call" of God on your life. Because there is a purpose for your life, and by the supernatural impartation voice of the Lord, it must be accomplished.

Again, in the Bible, we read about the Lord's voice:

> The boy Samuel ministered before the LORD under Eli. In those days the word of the LORD was rare; there were not many visions. One night Eli, whose eyes were becoming so weak that he could barely see, was lying down in his usual

place. The lamp of God had not yet gone out, and Samuel was lying down in the temple of the LORD, where the ark of God was. Then the LORD called Samuel. Samuel answered, "Here I am." And he ran to Eli and said, "Here I am; you called me."

But Eli said, "I did not call; go back and lie down."

So he went and lay down. Again the LORD called, "Samuel!"

And Samuel got up and went to Eli and said, "Here I am; you called me."

"My son," Eli said, "I did not call; go back and lie down."

Now Samuel did not yet know the LORD: The word of the LORD had not yet been revealed to him. The LORD called Samuel a third time, and Samuel got up and went to Eli and said, "Here I am; you called me." Then Eli realized that the LORD was calling the boy.

So Eli told Samuel, "Go and lie down, and if he calls you, say, 'Speak, LORD, for your servant is listening.'" So Samuel went and lay down in his place.

The LORD came and stood there, calling as at the other times, "Samuel! Samuel!"

Then Samuel said, "Speak, for your servant is listening."

And the LORD said to Samuel: "See, I am about to do something in Israel that will make the ears of everyone who hears of it tingle. At that time I will carry out against Eli everything I spoke against his family—from beginning to end. For I told him that I would judge his family for ever because of the sin he knew about; his sons made themselves contemptible and he failed to restrain them. Therefore, I swore to the house of Eli, 'The guilt of Eli's house will never be atoned for by sacrifice or offering.'" Samuel lay down until morning and then opened the doors of the house of the LORD.

He was afraid to tell Eli the vision, but Eli called him and said, "Samuel, my son."

Samuel answered, "Here I am."

"What was it he said to you?" Eli asked. "Do not hide it from me. May God deal with you, be it ever so severely, if you hide from me anything he told you." So Samuel told him everything, hiding nothing from him. Then Eli said, "He is the LORD; let him do what is good in his eyes." The LORD was with Samuel as he grew up, and let none of his words fall to the ground (1 Samuel 3:1-19).

How interesting the call of Prophet Samuel in the Bible is! He was called at a tender age, when he knew nothing about the call of God. However, of course because of the supernatural impartation of the Lord's voice, his life became a fulfillment; in other words, the purpose of his destiny was accomplished.

I hope you are enjoying the deep revelations of the Holy Spirit.

But I would love for you to focus with me on Prophet Isaiah in the Bible.

> Then I heard the voice of the LORD saying, "Who shall I send? And who will go for us?"
>
> And I said, "Here am I. Send me!"
>
> He said, "Go and tell this people: 'Be ever hearing, but never understanding; be ever seeing, but never perceiving.'" (Isaiah 6:8-9)

Reading the scriptures of Isaiah, we know Isaiah was a prophet, but there came a time in his ministry when he reached the climax of his prophesies. He heard the voice of the Lord as the Bible makes it clear, and he was able to tell God that he was totally ready to accomplish the purpose of his destiny. He told God he was willing to go, so God should send him.

Isn't this wonderful, the voice of the Lord fulfills your life? And with the voice of the Lord, you totally come into a realization that you have a purpose in your life, so you become prepared and ready to accomplish what your destiny demands.

Chapter Four

The Voice of Jesus Christ

*C*HILDREN OF GOD, I want us to understand that even that we talk and people listen is a gift. It doesn't have to be just preaching the word of God or being comedians or listening to musics, but I believe people have good words and wise sayings and all this cometh with voice.

In fact, I love the history of Jesus Christ, the son of our living God who came before us. In him, all things were made; without him nothing was made that has been made. But, my fellow believers, I hope we have all been convinced by the deep revelations of the Holy Spirit that our "King of Kings" Jesus came to earth in human form, but he wasn't human made.

The Bible tells of the existence of "Jesus Christ," the son of the living God on earth.

> In the sixth month, God sent the angel Gabriel to Nazareth, a town in Galilee, to a virgin pledged to be married to a man

named Joseph, a descendant of David. The virgin's name was Mary. The angel went to her and said, "Greetings, you who are highly favored! The Lord is with you." Mary was greatly troubled at his words and wondered what kind of greeting this might be.

But the angel said to her, "Do not be afraid, Mary, you have found favor with God. You will be with child and give birth to a son, and you are to give him the name Jesus. He will be great and will be called the Son of the Most High. The Lord God will give him the throne of his father David, and he will reign over the house of Jacob forever; his kingdom will never end."

"How will this be," Mary asked the angel, "since I am a virgin?"

The angel answered, "The Holy Spirit will come upon you, and the power of the Most High will overshadow you. So the holy one to be born will be called the son of God. Even Elizabeth your relative is going to have a child in her old age, and she who was said to be barren is in her sixth month. For nothing is impossible with God."

"I am the Lord's servant," Mary answered. "May it be to me as you have said." Then the angel left her. (Luke 1:26-38).

What a marvelous, wonderful, and powerful transition! I hope we all knew that story.

God sent an angel whose name was Gabriel to a virgin called Mary. And the angel proclaimed to her that she would bring forth a divine son, who would be the savior of the world.

In other words, the angel carried the *voice* of the Lord to Mary; the birth of *Jesus Christ* wasn't Angel Gabriel's decision. Believers, the angel declared unto the virgin and she conceived; this is beyond thinking. How can this be possible in the natural world we live in? I believe the God we serve is a supernatural God and He makes the impossible possible.

Brothers and Sisters, would you agree with me that voice is a spirit and that's why it is supernatural? In this situation, the voice of God spoken through the angel became a seed in the womb of the virgin and she conceived.

And in the story, we recognize that the impartation of the Holy Spirit and the power of God that the angel released on the Virgin Mary activated the supernatural voice of the Lord that had been placed in the Virgin Mary.

Believers, I need you to think deeply about this revelation; if there were no voice, how would this have been possible? Our voice is very important. I declare to you Christians, our voice is supernatural and we need to respect it and begin to perform with our voices. This is a proof to you that without voice, there would be no activity under the sun.

You know, as you read earlier, the voice of the Lord came forth to accomplish great things. Now Jesus Christ, our savior, was born, not by human means, but by the supernatural power of the Most High God, which was accomplished through the voice (message) of God carried to a virgin called Mary by Angel Gabriel.

And the Lord himself affirmed Jesus as his son in the Bible:

> As soon as Jesus was baptized, he went up out of the water. At that moment heaven was opened, and he saw the spirit of God descending like a dove and lighting on him. And a voice from heaven said, "This is my son, whom I love; with him I am well pleased." (Matthew 3:16-17)

We can get an affirmation on this story in the following passage:

> A voice came from the cloud, saying, "This is my son, whom I have chosen; listen to him." When the voice had spoken, they found that Jesus was alone.

> The disciples kept this to themselves, and told no one at that time what they had seen. (Luke 9:35-36)

Believers, these two affirmations of the Lord's *voice* concerning Jesus Christ truthfully certify the proclamation of the message (voice) carried to the virgin Mary by the angel Gabriel.

In fact, believers, this message is beyond thoughts, and I have had to go through sleepless nights on several occasions to comprehend the deep revelations the Holy Spirit was revealing to me. And I want to confirm that it was also the voice of the Lord talking to me that made me able to write this book.

But before we continue with the operating or manifestation *voice* of Jesus Christ, I would love for us to get another deep revelation about a great prophet of God from the Bible.

When the Bible foretold his birth, he was introduced or described as: *"A voice of one calling: 'In the desert, prepare the way for the LORD, make straight in the wilderness a highway for our God'" (Isaiah 40:3).*

The man who prophesies about this voice was the prophet Isaiah from the Old Testament. He was one of the greatest prophets of the Lord from the Old Testament, and his prophesy about this voice came into fulfillment in the New Testament.

> This is he who was spoken of through the prophet Isaiah: "A voice of one calling in the desert, 'Prepare the way for the LORD, make straight paths for him.'" (Matthew 3:3)

My fellow Christians, why would the Bible describe someone as a voice? If you look at the above scripture, you will find that this voice the Bible is talking about was a human being! John the Baptist was being described as a voice. I believe a voice is really something we should pay great attention to.

Believers, I think I did say earlier that anytime the Lord voices something, it comes into accomplishment. Now we just noticed how God voiced something through a prophet in the Old Testament, and it came into fulfillment in the New Testament.

This *voice* was John the Baptist, who also carried the voice of the Lord concerning his only begotten son Jesus Christ, who also came into fulfillment in the New Testament.

Now if you have ever read the story of John the Baptist, you know that his story is very fascinating. For the Bible made it clear that the purpose of this prophet of God, John the Baptist, was to prepare the way and make straight paths for the coming of Jesus Christ, so he left home at a very tender age to dwell in caves in the desert.

He ate nothing except locusts and wild honey; his clothes were made of camel hair, and he had a leather belt around his waist. John the Baptist preached in the desert about salvation (Jesus Christ). People went out to him confessing their sins, and he baptized many of them in the Jordan River.

Believers, there was something special and marvelous about this man's ministry, which I observed and made me feel overwhelmed. I believe we all accept the fact that our appearance says a lot about our personality and that before you can stand before people in high places and positions, you must look good in your outward appearance. But with this man of God (John the Baptist), it was his voice that attracted so many people to him, both high and low.

The Bible said many people from Jerusalem—kings, priests, soldiers, and tax collectors—came to listen to his voice, but he wasn't dressed in fine garments, nor was any fragrance or oil used on him, and yet he could still accomplish the purpose of his destiny.

At this point, I want you to realize that your voice can attract queens, kings, priests, and presidents to listen to you. Your supernatural gift (*voice*) can draw people from very high places and positions to you and you don't need to wait for any luxurious clothes or ornaments before you begin to manifest in your voice.

Brothers and Sisters, with the revelations in this book, I want to make it clear to you that there is no gift or talent in this world that you don't need a voice to manifest or operate.

But I would say by the grace of our Lord God Almighty, you all have this supernatural gift, so you need to arise and shine.

Jesus Christ began his ministry at the age of twelve, but he started preaching (evangelizing) at the age of thirty. We notice that at this tender age of twelve years, he sneaked into a temple and involved himself by starting a conversation with the priests, elders, and teachers of the Law of Moses.

Now the secret is, at that time, he was activating his voice with his communication skills. He began preaching (evangelizing) to the people of Jerusalem, and by his anointed voice, he attracted to him his twelve disciples; there were many people who followed him but weren't recommended as his disciples.

"From that time on Jesus began to preach, 'Repent for the kingdom of heaven is near'" (Matthew 4:17).

"On the last and greatest day of the Feast, Jesus stood and said in a loud voice, 'If anyone is thirsty, let him come to me, as the Scripture has said, streams of living water will flow within him'" (John 7:37-38).

Jesus, with his supernatural voice, prayed and also taught his disciples how to pray. We find out in the Bible that he did many miracles, signs, and wonders; healed the sick; and raised the dead.

Right now, I want you to ask yourself how could Jesus do all these things that he did if it wasn't by his voice. Let me just hammer on how Jesus raised Lazarus from the dead.

> Now a man named Lazarus was sick. He was from Bethany, the village of Mary and her sister Martha. This Mary, whose brother Lazarus now lay sick, was the same one who poured perfume on the Lord and wiped his feet with her hair. So the sisters sent word to Jesus, "Lord, the one you love is sick."

> When he heard this, Jesus said, "This sickness will not end in death. No, it is for God's glory so that God's son may be glorified through it." Jesus loved Martha and her sister and Lazarus.

> Yet when he heard that Lazarus was sick, he stayed where he was two more days. Then he said to his disciples, "Let us go back to Judea."

> "But Rabbi," they said, "a short while ago the Jews tried to stone you, and yet you are going back there?"

> Jesus answered, "Are there not twelve hours of daylight? A man who walks by day will not stumble, for he sees by this world's light. It is when he walks by night that he stumbles, for he has no light." After he had said this, he went on to tell them, "Our friend Lazarus has fallen asleep; but I am going there to wake him up."

> His disciples replied, "Lord, if he sleeps, he will get better."

Jesus had been speaking of his death, but his disciples thought he meant natural sleep. So then he told them plainly, "Lazarus is dead, and for your sake I am glad I was not there, so that you may believe. But let us go to him."

Then Thomas (called Didymus) said to the rest of the disciples, "Let us also go, that we may die with him."

On his arrival, Jesus found that Lazarus had already been in the tomb four days. Bethany was less than two miles from Jerusalem, and many Jews had come to Martha and Mary to comfort them in the loss of their brother.

When Martha heard that Jesus was coming, she went out to meet him, but Mary stayed at home. "Lord," Martha said to Jesus, "if you had been here, my brother would not have died. But I know that even now God will give you whatever you ask."

Jesus said to her, "Your brother will rise again."

Martha answered, "I know he will rise again in the resurrection at the last day."

Jesus said to her, "I am the resurrection and the life. He who believes in me will live, even though he dies; and whoever lives and believes in me will never die. Do you believe this?"

"Yes, Lord," she told him, "I believe that you are the Christ, the son of God, who was to come into the world."

And after she had said this, she went back and called her sister Mary aside. "The Teacher is here," she said, "and is asking for you." When Mary heard this, she got up quickly and went to him. Now Jesus had not yet entered the village, but was still at the place where Martha had met him.

When the Jews who had been with Mary in the house, comforting her, noticed how quickly she got up and went out, they followed her, supposing she was going to the tomb to mourn there. When Mary reached the place where Jesus was and saw him, she fell at his feet and said, "Lord, if you had been here, my brother would not have died."

When Jesus saw her weeping and the Jews who had come along with her also weeping, he was deeply moved in spirit and troubled. "Where have you laid him?" he asked.

"Come and see, Lord," they replied.

Jesus wept.

Then the Jews said, "See how he loved him!"

But some of them said, "Could not he who opened the eyes of the blind man have kept this man from dying?"

Jesus, once more deeply moved, came to the tomb. It was a cave with a stone laid across the entrance. "Take away the stone," he said.

"But, Lord," said Martha, the sister of the dead man, "by this time there is a bad odor, for he has been there four days."

Then Jesus said, "Did I not tell you that if you believed, you would see the glory of God?" So they took away the stone. Then Jesus looked up and said, "Father, I thank you that you have heard me. I knew that you always hear me, but I said this for the benefit of the people standing here, that they may believe that you sent me."

When he had said this, Jesus called in a loud voice, "Lazarus, come out!" The dead man came out, his hands and feet wrapped with strips of linen, and a cloth around his face. Jesus said to them, "Take off the grave clothes and let him go." (John 11:1-44).

In fact, Believers, this is very powerful: with a loud and an attracting voice, a dead person gone for four days could come to life.

But the Bible tells us even more stories about Jesus raising dead people, and his disciples did the same. So, we know that with our voice, we can also raise the dead if only we know how to present it and persevere humbly before God. We can also gain recognition and identification before the Lord with our voice.

Praise the Lord. My brothers and sisters, I want you to acknowledge something from the scriptures, which the Holy Spirit revealed to me. This is how demons have possessed our lives; if you are the type who can't talk, you must speak or use your voice to do something. This is especially for those who find it pretty okay to describe themselves as "shy people," those who say, "I am timid and can't stand before too many people. I fear to stand in front of people to talk, pray, sing, or preach. The Bible makes it clear that such people are demon possessed. Jesus once said to his disciples,

I tell you, whoever acknowledges me before men, the son of Man will also acknowledge him before the angels of God. But he who disowns me before men will be disowned before the angels of God. (Luke 12:8-9)

And also to let you know, when you are timid, you definitely have the spirit of pride hidden in you. Just imagine, right after the pastor gave the closing prayers and dismissed the congregation, instead greeting someone, shake hands with or hug a brother or sister, you just walk out to your car and drive home. Why? Because you feel so proud of yourself, but you think you are shy. I tell you the truth; you need to check the pride spirit in you.

Believers, it is not good to be shy; rather, you should prove yourself wrong. Other people are doing it, and you must also do it and be successful.

Let's read a story of Jesus Christ who once healed a man who was mute and deaf.

While they were going out, a man who was demon-possessed and could not talk was brought to Jesus. And when the demon was driven out, the man who had been mute spoke. The crowd was amazed and said, "Nothing like this has ever been seen in Israel." (Matthew 9:32-33)

Now, Believers, if you could agree with me, the Bible deliberately makes us aware that the mute man spoke because the demons were driven out. Let me just use this opportunity to make you aware that it is the demons that are preventing you from gaining wealth (riches). Because they know when you are able to stand before people to voice your talents (gifts), you will become a multimillionaire. And Christians always go to prophets, pastors, and men of God to be delivered from generational and ancestral curses that they are fighting in their lives, not knowing that it is their voice that is under that great curse.

From this moment, I want you to cast out those demons that are holding you back from making your dreams come true, because your destiny needs a fulfillment, so you need to voice out your purpose in this journey of life.

Jesus once performed a magnificent miracle. It was not something he needed to touch or see; he just spoke the word with his supernatural voice, and it was done at the same time he proclaimed the miracle or the healing.

Let's read from the Bible:

> After the two days he left for Galilee. (Now Jesus himself had pointed out that a prophet has no honor in his own country.) When he arrived in Galilee, the Galileans welcomed him. They had seen all that he had done in Jerusalem at the Passover Feast, for they also had been there.
>
> Once more he visited Cana in Galilee, where he had turned the water into wine. And there was a certain royal official

whose son lay sick at Capernaum. When this man heard that Jesus had arrived in Galilee from Judea, he went to him and begged him to come and heal his son, who was close to death. "Unless you people see miraculous signs and wonders," Jesus told him, "you will never believe."

The royal official said, "Sir, come down before my child dies."

Jesus replied, "You may go. Your son will live."

The man took Jesus at his word and departed. While he was still on the way, his servants met him with the news that his boy was living. When he enquired as to the time when his son got better, they said to him, "The fever left him yesterday at the seventh hour."

Then the father realized that this was the exact time at which Jesus had said to him, "Your son will live." So he and his entire household believed. This was the second miraculous sign that Jesus performed, having come from Judea to Galilee. (John 4:43-54)

Praise the Lord! My fellow believers, as we read the story, we notice that Jesus voiced a proclamation to a royal official whose son was sick. And the story helps us understand that at the same time Jesus spoke to the royal official, his son was healed. Isn't this unbelievable? My brothers and sisters, I want you to be happy about this supernatural gift the Lord has also given to you. Rise up and begin to move in your voice!

My fellow Christians, I know at times you might want to do something with your voice, but the people around you rebuke you and insult you, but please, I want to encourage you and tell you that the more insults aimed at you, the more you should voice your supernatural giftings, which the Lord has deposited in you.

Another miracle happened to a blind man in the Bible.

> As Jesus approached Jericho, a blind man was sitting by the roadside begging. When he heard the crowd going by, he asked what was happening. They told him, "Jesus of Nazareth is passing by."
>
> He called out, "Jesus, Son of David, have mercy on me!"
>
> Those who led the way rebuked him and told him to be quiet, but he shouted all the more, "Son of David, have mercy on me!"
>
> Jesus stopped and ordered the man to be brought to him. When he came near, Jesus asked him, "What do you want me to do for you?"
>
> "Lord, I want to see," he replied.
>
> Jesus said to him, "Receive your sight; your faith has healed you." Immediately he received his sight and followed Jesus, praising God. When all the people saw it, they also praised God. (Luke 18:35-43)

I hope this story will encourage you. The blind beggar was rebuked by the people around him, but he never gave up, and Jesus recognized his voice. I urge you to continue to voice your gifting until the Lord gives you the answer that suits your situation: the money you are looking for to establish that business, that marriage you want it to stand, you should voice them out to God.

Believers, I need you to understand and perceive that there is nothing done on earth without the supernatural voice of our God Almighty, and by his loving kindness and grace, he has deposited this power of voice in us. The Lord has given each of you a voice; it is your choice to make a noise in every aspect of your life so that you can succeed. We pray with our voice, talk with our voice, sing with our voice, and preach with our voice—every talent introduced on earth is accomplished by voice.

As I was reading through the Bible, the Holy Spirit was showing me that the miracles, healings, signs, wonders, praying, preaching, and prophesies were accompanied by *voice*.

I want us to see quickly how Jesus shouted the devil up with his voice during his ministry on earth when Satan tried to convince Jesus and threaten Jesus's life with his (Satan's) voice.

But the glory is to God that Jesus is the one; in him, every creature's voice was made, so he can distinguish between voices from God and voices that are not from God but from the devil.

According to the Bible, the devil (Satan) tried several times to convince Jesus, the son of the Most High God, to worship him (Satan).

Then Jesus was led by the spirit into the desert to be tempted by the devil. After fasting for forty days and forty nights, he was hungry. The tempter came to him and said, "If you are the Son of God, tell these stones to become bread."

Jesus answered, "It is written: 'Man does not live on bread alone, but on every word that comes from the mouth of God.'"

Then the devil took him to the holy city and had him stand on the highest point of the temple. "If you are the Son of God," he said, "throw yourself down. For it is written: 'He will command his angels concerning you, and they will lift you up in their hands, so that you will not strike your foot against a stone.'"

Jesus answered him, "It is also written: 'Do not put the Lord your God to the test.'"

Again, the devil took him to a very high mountain and showed him all the kingdoms of the world and their splendor. "All this I will give you," he said, "if you will bow down and worship me."

Jesus said to him, "Away from me, Satan! For it is written: 'Worship the Lord your God, and serve him only.'"

Then the devil left him, and angels came and attended him. (Matthew 4:1-11)

But Jesus recognized him and defeated him (Satan). Believers, how I hope you are deeply convinced about your voice, what you can really build, establish, and accomplish in life with your voice.

I also remember from the Bible another incident in the life of Jesus and his disciples. Once they were crossing over a lake to the other side, but the devil threatened them with a wild storm (blowing waves), and immediately the disciples woke Jesus up because he was sleeping. Jesus awoke and shouted at the wind.

> One day Jesus said to his disciples, "Let's go over to the other side of the lake." So they got into a boat and set out. As they sailed, he fell asleep. A squall came down on the lake, so that the boat was being swamped, and they were in great danger.
>
> The disciples went and woke him, saying, "Master, Master, we're going to drown!"
>
> He got up and rebuked the wind and the raging waters; the storm subsided, and all was calm. "Where is your faith?" he asked his disciples.
>
> In fear and amazement they asked one another, "Who is this? He commands even the winds and the water, and they obey him." (Luke 8:22-25)

Brothers and Sisters, I want to push you to the conclusion that you can do something with this supernatural gift, for faith comes from what is heard and what comes through the word of Christ.

"Consequently, faith comes from hearing the message, and the message is heard through the word of Christ" (Romans 10:17).

Believers, I want to ask, what do we hear with our ears? Isn't it *voices?*

It is my prayer, after reading this revelatory knowledge, that the spirit of the Lord will impart into you a refreshing, renewal, and restoration of the supernatural voice God has deposited in your life, so you can come out of yourself and shine. And your voice will take you to places you have never been.

Before I end the chapter on the voice of *Jesus Christ*, let's enjoy the story of how a sinful man is saved by his humble voice even at the point of his death.

> Jesus said, "Father, forgive them, for they do not know what they are doing." And they divided up his clothes by casting lots.
>
> The people stood watching, and the rulers even sneered at him. They said, "He saved others; let him save himself if he is the Christ of God, the Chosen One."
>
> The soldiers also came up and mocked him. They offered him wine vinegar and said, "If you are the king of the Jews, save yourself." There was a written notice above him, which read: THIS IS THE KING OF THE JEWS.
>
> One of the criminals who hung there hurled insults at him: "Aren't you the Christ? Save yourself and us!"

But the other criminal rebuked him. "Don't you fear God," he said, "since you are under the same sentence? We are punished justly, for we are getting what our deeds deserve. But this man has done nothing wrong."

Then he said, "Jesus, remember me when you come into your kingdom."

Jesus answered him, "I tell you the truth, today you will be with me in paradise." (Luke 23:34-43)

Believers, how could two men see the same Jesus and one choose to mock him with his voice and the other choose to pray to him with his humble voice? I don't know, but they did. When one prayed with his voice, Jesus recognized him and his humble voice, and Jesus loved him enough to save him.

My fellows Christians, do you see how your voice can bring salvation to your life?

I need you to allow the Holy Spirit to work on your voice from this point, for your blessing is in installments waiting for you to activate it with your voice.

Jesus left the scene after he was taken up to heaven, and he gave a mission to his disciples, the mission of preaching salvation to the world. Therefore, we are also responsible for accomplishing the same mission in all the nations.

One will ask, "What is the mission?" Believers, the mission is preaching (evangelizing), praying, prophesying, healing, and performing miracles, signs, and wonders, and this can be fulfilled with the power of our voice through the word of the Lord.

This reminds me of the disciples. Jesus had been taken up to heaven, and it was their turn to carry on with the mission. Believers, I hope we remember that the first thing they did to manifest in their voices was to come together in prayer to God.

> On their release, Peter and John went back to their own people and reported all that the chief priest and elders had said to them. When they heard this, they raised their voices together in prayer to God. "Sovereign Lord," they said, "you made the heaven and the earth and the sea, and everything in them. You spoke by the Holy Spirit through the mouth of your servant, our father David: 'Why do the nations rage and the people plot in vain? And the rulers gather together against the Lord and against his Anointed One.' Indeed Herod and Pontius Pilate met together with the Gentiles and the people of Israel in this city to conspire against your holy servant Jesus, whom you anointed. They did what your power and will had decided beforehand should happen. Now, Lord, consider their threats and enable your servants to speak your word with great boldness. Stretch out your hand to heal and perform miraculous signs and wonders through the name of your holy servant Jesus."

After they prayed, the place where they were meeting was shaken. And they were all filled with the Holy Spirit and spoke the word of God boldly. (Acts 4:23-31)

And, Believers, the Bible makes it clear that the earth shook, because their voices had been recognized by the Lord. These prayers were answered, and their gifting and talents began to manifest.

Isn't this awesome? If you can confidently believe in your voice and rise up to your feet in prayer, tell God to remember you, recognize your voice, and activate your talents within you so that they can come out to life. Little did you know you could also pray for the earth to shake?

Believers, your time has come, and it is now.God did it, and Jesus has done it. Jesus's prophets and disciples are doing it, and we as his followers can also do it and must do it.

Once again during the ministry of Jesus's disciples, we see the power of voice make manifest in their lives:

> One day Peter and John were going up to the temple at the time of prayer—at three in the afternoon. Now a man crippled from birth was being carried to the temple gate called Beautiful, where he was put every day to beg from those going into the temple courts. When he saw Peter and John about to enter, he asked them for money. Peter looked straight at him, as did John. Then Peter said, "Look at us!" So the man gave them his attention, expecting to get something from them.

> Then Peter said, "Silver or gold I do not have, but what I have I give you. In the name of Jesus Christ of Nazareth, walk." Taking him by the right hand, he helped him up, and instantly the man's feet and ankles became strong. He

jumped to his feet and began to walk. Then he went with them into the temple courts, walking and jumping, and praising God.

When all the people saw him walking and praising God, they recognized him as the same man who used to sit begging at the temple gate called Beautiful, and they were filled with wonder and amazement at what had happened to him. (Acts 3:1-10)

Now, with the above story, we can gladly testify to where the supernatural voice in the disciples is taking them; you should carefully study the above story. With the power invested in Peter, which came out with his voice, he restored a crippled beggar to his feet.

Believer, I may not know what the devil has bound you with, but I know that's why you can't operate with your voice. It may be fear, shyness, or the spirit of timidity. I myself used to be timid, but with the supernatural revelations I got through this book, I can confidently tell you am no more.

I remember when I used to be afraid to stand before my colleagues in class when I was in college, but not now; by his grace, I can stand before congregations and pray, counsel elderly people, and also prophesy onto people's lives.

And what an honor it is when people see you as a superstar when all you are doing is manifesting the talent God has deposited in you, which your voice is doing the work.

Now there is an amazing story in the Bible of another unrighteous man whose name was Saul but was later changed to Paul. This man was not even a disciple, Jesus trained. He was filled with a stubborn spirit, and his mission was to torment and persecute God's children. I hope we can remember this man.

But the Bible makes it clear that through the voice of Jesus, he suddenly changed and became one of God's disciples.

Meanwhile, Saul was still breathing out murderous threats against the Lord's disciples. He went to the high priest and asked him for letters to the synagogues in Damascus, so that if he found any there who belonged to the way, whether men or women, he might take them as prisoners to Jerusalem. As he neared Damascus on his journey, suddenly a light from heaven flashed around him.

He fell to the ground and heard a voice say to him, "Saul, Saul, why do you persecute me?"

"Who are you, Lord?" Saul asked.

"I am Jesus, whom you are persecuting," he replied. "Now get up and go into the city, and you will be told what you must do." The men travelling with Saul stood there speechless; they heard the sound but did not see anyone. Saul got up from the ground, but when he opened his eyes he could see nothing. So they led him by the hand into Damascus. For three days he was blind, and did not eat or drink anything. In Damascus there was a disciple named Ananias.

The Lord called to him in a vision, "Ananias!"

"Yes, Lord," he answered.

The Lord told him, "Go to the house of Judas on Straight Street and ask for a man from Tarsus named Saul, for he is praying. In a vision he has seen a man named Ananias come and place his hands on him to restore his sight."

"Lord," Ananias answered, "I have heard many reports about this man and all the harm he has done to your saints in Jerusalem. And he has come here with authority from the chief priest to arrest all who call on your name."

But the Lord said to Ananias, "Go! This man is my chosen instrument to carry my name before the Gentiles and their kings and before the people of Israel. I will show him how much he must suffer for my name."

Then Ananias went to the house and entered it. Placing his hands on Saul, he said, "Brother Saul, the Lord—Jesus, who appeared to you on the road as you were coming here—has sent me so that you may see again and be filled with the Holy Spirit." Immediately, something like scales fell from Saul's eyes, and he could see again. He got up and was baptized, and after taking some food, he regained his strength. Saul spent several days with the disciples in Damascus.

At once he began to preach in the synagogues that Jesus is the Son of God. All those who heard him were astonished and asked, "Isn't he the man who caused havoc in Jerusalem among those who call on this name? And hasn't he come here to take them as prisoners to the chief priests?" Yet Saul grew more and more powerful and battled the Jews living in Damascus by proving that Jesus is the Christ.

After many days had gone by, the Jews conspired to kill him, but Saul learned of their plan. Day and night they kept close watch on the city gates in order to kill him. But his followers took him by night and lowered him in a basket through an opening in the wall. When he came to Jerusalem, he tried to join the disciples, but they were all afraid of him, not believing that he really was a disciple. But Barnabas took him and brought him to the apostles.

He told them how Saul on his journey had seen the Lord and that the Lord had spoken to him, and how in Damascus he had preached fearlessly in the name of Jesus. So Saul stayed with them and moved about freely in Jerusalem, speaking boldly in the name of the Lord. He talked and debated with the Grecian Jews, but they tried to kill him.

When the brothers learned of this, they took him down to Caesarea and sent him off to Tarsus. Then the church throughout Judea, Galilee and Samaria enjoyed a time of peace. It was strengthened; and encouraged by the Holy Spirit; it grew in numbers, living in the fear of the Lord. (Acts 9:1-31).

I love this supernatural voice of *Jesus Christ*. The voice of Jesus changed the actions of a man who was on a mission of negativity and evil. The voice of the Lord changed his mission from negativities to possitivities.

Believers that means, by one's voice, one can change the plans and works of the enemy (negetivities) into possitivities.

Isn't this even more awesome than what we expect?

Think about this, my fellow brothers and sisters in Christ, the Lord God Almighty has given us a great privilege to be divinely blessed (rich) from everlasting to everlasting.

Also remember that even if we die, our voice still lives, because our soul has the voice too; that is why the Bible makes us understand from the book of Revelation that the voices of the righteous souls are crying out to the LORD, asking when the Lord is going to bring judgment on the earth.

> When he opened the fifth seal, I saw under the altar the souls of those who had been slain because of the word of God and the testimony they had maintained. They called out in a loud voice, "How long, Sovereign Lord, holy and true, until you judge the inhabitants of the earth and avenge our blood?" (Revelation 6:9-10)

Believers, this is to encourage you and help you understand that with your voice, you can become whoever you really want to be. The choice is yours whether you will use it righteously or unrighteously, humbly or proudly.

Saul, who became Paul, became so powerful in operating with his voice. He healed the sick, did many miracles, cast out demons, and even raised the dead.

Now there was this particular powerful manifestation about his ministry which I would like us to elaborate on.

Apostle Paul became so powerful that after his preaching, miracles, signs, and wonders follow, and the people even tried to use his aprons and handkerchiefs to do miracles. God did extraordinary miracles through Paul, even handkerchiefs and aprons that had touched him were taken to the sick and their illnesses were cured and evil spirits left them.

> Some Jews who went around driving out evil spirits tried to invoke the name of the Lord Jesus over those who were demon-possessed.

> They would say, "In the name of Jesus, whom Paul preaches, I command you to come out." Seven sons of Sceva, a Jewish chief priest, were doing this. One day the evil spirit answered them, "Jesus I know and I know about Paul, but who are you?" Then the man who had the evil spirit jumped on them and overpowered them all. He gave them such a beating that they ran out of the house naked and bleeding.

> When this became known to the Jews and Greeks living in Ephesus, they were all seized with fear, and the name of the Lord Jesus was held in high honor. Many of those who believed now came and openly confessed their evil deeds.

A number who had practiced sorcery brought their scrolls
together and burned them publicly.

When they calculated the value of the scrolls, the total came
to fifty thousand drachmas. In this way the word of the
Lord spread widely and grew in power. (Acts 19:11-20)

Just imagine the marvelous, powerful miracles the Lord made Paul
do, but what interests me is the Jews who went around driving out
demons with the name of Jesus and the apostle Paul. But funnily
enough, the demons recognized their voices and said to them,
"Jesus I know and Paul we know, but who are you?"

Oh, wow! Isn't this magnificent? Demons also recognized voices,
so the demons identified the voices of the Jews because their voices
were not appropriate before God, the demons jumped on them
and flogged them.

Believers, this is to let you testify that if you don't use your voice
appropriately, it can lead to your destruction. But fair enough,
Jesus loved us so much and has given us these supernatural gifts
to tap into our blessings. The choice is yours to use it humbly or
proudly, but always remember that the voice of the proud is not
pleasing in the sight of the Lord. And children of God I hope we
have got the picture also understand the deep revelation the Holy
Spirit is teaching us.

Precious one will you agree with me that it is the supernatural voice
behind the powerful word of God Almighty that brings healing,
miracles, signs and wonders to us. With all the miracles that took
place during the time of Jesus and even in the life of the disciples

we realized that it is their voice behind the word of God that cause healing and deliverance to the dead, cripple, blind, lame, demon possessed mute, deaf and dump. Please this is to encourage you child of God reading this book; you might be a disable, slave to sin or even cripple in your marriage, finances, business or in your life also people might be describing you as invalid (outcast) but Please I encourage you right now that you only need to voice out to God for him to hear your prayer, cry and groaning and I guarantee you that you will be touched in every part of your life if you present and preserve your voice humbly before Him.

Chapter Five

Marriage

*P*EOPLE OF GOD, Marriage; from the beginning of the world or creation has been a broad decision and a tough situation for Mankind. Marriage is the sweetest and at the same time the most challenging stage in mankind's life.

With my best of knowledge and deep revelations I believe there are three things which are very important for mankind to consider in one's life. These are the three important stages of one's life and I believe mankind need to consider and fulfil them. I called these three things 'THE THREE M(s)', which is MASTER—MISSION & MATE.

> ➢ MASTER—Your creator that's God Almighty

> ➢ MISSION—Your purpose in this universe

> ➢ MATE—Your partner (Marriage)

Believers mankind can never missed or by pass the above mentioned stages and be a true survival in this life. For you to be a real human and survive the process of life I believe that mankind should first know his **MASTER**—that's your creator who brought you into this world. Secondly, your **MISSION**—which is our purpose in this world, we need to know why we are here and what we must accomplish before we leave here and thirdly, your **MATE**—which is your partner these is the time you need to be initiated with some one for you two to procreate because of what God said to mankind after creation.

So God created man in his own image, in the image of God he created him; male and female he created them.
God blessed them and said to them "Be fruitful and increase in number; fill the earth and subdue it. Rule over the fish of the sea and the birds of the air and over every living creature that moves on the ground. (Genesis 1:27-28)

God Proposed to mankind to give birth or procreate to fill the surface of the earth like the sand at the sea shore for creation to move on. But brothers and sisters with all the stages of life I have realized that during the stage of marriage that's having your mate has been the sweetest but the most challenging stage of mankind's life.

I believe that, this stage even carries sixty five percent (65%) of mankind's life therefore mankind need to be very careful of whom you choose as your mate because after getting married and at the end of it all you realized you are with the wrong mate this means you have wasted sixty five percent (65%) of your life away.

But I tell you not to let this discourage or makes you afraid of getting married or enter into marriage that is why Apostle

Paul makes us aware from the Holy Scriptures in the book of Corinthians.

But if you do marry, you have not sinned; and if a virgin marries, she has not sinned. But those who marry will face many troubles in this Life and I want to spare you with this. (1corothians 7:28)

Precious one there is one thing I want us to know, which is; we must understand that mankind was formed and created out of Clay (SAND). Therefore if a man and a woman is getting married there should be a total understanding that it is two different clay (SAND) which is about to be mixed together and you can only mix two clay's together by adding water to make them wet or soft before it gets to each other until you can't separate them anymore.

That's why the Lord made us understand from the Holy Scriptures that's "a man shall leave his family and be united with the wife and they shall become one flesh"

"Haven't you read," he replied, "That at the beginning the Creator 'made them male and female,' and said, 'For this reason a man will leave his father and mother and be united to his wife, and the two will become one flesh'? So they are no longer two, but one.

Therefore what God has joined together, let man not separate . . . . I tell you that anyone who divorces his wife, except for marital unfaithfulness, and marries another woman commits adultery." (Matthew 19:4-6, 9)

People of God if something should become one you can not separate it, anytime you try to separate it; it will tear each apart.

Believers this description or illustration is to let you beware that marriage is not a stage or a platform you can climb anyhow you want or get down anyhow you want. During this process in one's life is a stage which should be handled with cautiousness, maturity and a life time decision.

Even the bible declares to us that we should let our Yes be yes and our No be No, else anything beyond it; is evil.

Simple let your 'Yes' be 'Yes', and 'No' be 'No'; anything beyond this Comes from the evil one' (Matthew 5:37)

Believers, divorce is an evil decision for mankind to make and separation is very detestable to God therefore we must understand that ONE means UNITY so if separation comes between something united instantly it begun to hate each other and this leads to unrighteousness or ungodliness. Please children of God, is not good to divorce your partner because God hate divorce;

"I hate divorce, Says the LORD God of Israel, and I hate a man's covering himself with violence as well with his garment". Says the LORD almighty. So guard yourself in your spirit and do not break faith (Malachi 2:16)

You know as a man of God, I have witness and counsel many people of their marriages and I know is not easy and never going to be easy for you at all from the day you enter into this initiation but my advice I always shared with my people; also with the deep revelation God has giving me about marriage is that, we must know and be very much aware in our lives that; definitely the one you love at times can hurt you so bad that you will feel like cursing, fighting, divorcing or separating but please this is the time for you to be strong and know that after every obstacle is a miracle.

May I use this opportunity to share this deep revelation with you; I hope we all remember the story about the death of Lazarus;

> Now a man named Lazarus was sick. He was from Bethany, the village of Mary and her sister Martha. This Mary, whose brother Lazarus now lay sick, was the same one who poured perfume on the Lord and wiped his feet with her hair. So the sisters sent word to Jesus, "Lord, the one you love is sick."
>
> When he heard this, Jesus said, "This sickness will not end in death. No, it is for God's glory so that God's son may be glorified through it." Jesus loved Martha and her sister and Lazarus.
>
> Yet when he heard that Lazarus was sick, he stayed where he was two more days. Then he said to his disciples, "Let us go back to Judea."
>
> "But Rabbi," they said, "a short while ago the Jews tried to stone you, and yet you are going back there?"
>
> Jesus answered, "Are there not twelve hours of daylight? A man who walks by day will not stumble, for he sees by this world's light. It is when he walks by night that he stumbles,

for he has no light." After he had said this, he went on to tell them, "Our friend Lazarus has fallen asleep; but I am going there to wake him up."

His disciples replied, "Lord, if he sleeps, he will get better."

Jesus had been speaking of his death, but his disciples thought he meant natural sleep. So then he told them plainly, "Lazarus is dead, and for your sake I am glad I was not there, so that you may believe. But let us go to him."

Then Thomas (called Didymus) said to the rest of the disciples, "Let us also go, that we may die with him."

On his arrival, Jesus found that Lazarus had already been in the tomb four days. Bethany was less than two miles from Jerusalem, and many Jews had come to Martha and Mary to comfort them in the loss of their brother.

When Martha heard that Jesus was coming, she went out to meet him, but Mary stayed at home. "Lord," Martha said to Jesus, "if you had been here, my brother would not have died. But I know that even now God will give you whatever you ask."

Jesus said to her, "Your brother will rise again."

Martha answered, "I know he will rise again in the resurrection at the last day."

Jesus said to her, "I am the resurrection and the life. He who believes in me will live, even though he dies; and whoever lives and believes in me will never die. Do you believe this?"

"Yes, Lord," she told him, "I believe that you are the Christ, the son of God, who was to come into the world." And after she had said this, she went back and called her sister Mary aside. "The Teacher is here," she said, "and is asking for you." When Mary heard this, she got up quickly and went to him. Now Jesus had not yet entered the village, but was still at the place where Martha had met him.

When the Jews who had been with Mary in the house, comforting her, noticed how quickly she got up and went out, they followed her, supposing she was going to the tomb to mourn there. When Mary reached the place where Jesus was and saw him, she fell at his feet and said, "Lord, if you had been here, my brother would not have died."

When Jesus saw her weeping and the Jews who had come along with her also weeping, he was deeply moved in spirit and troubled. "Where have you laid him?" he asked.

"Come and see, Lord," they replied.

Jesus wept.

Then the Jews said, "See how he loved him!"

But some of them said, "Could not he who opened the eyes of the blind man have kept this man from dying?"

Jesus, once more deeply moved, came to the tomb. It was a cave with a stone laid across the entrance. "Take away the stone," he said.

"But, Lord," said Martha, the sister of the dead man, "by this time there is a bad odor, for he has been there four days."

Then Jesus said, "Did I not tell you that if you believed, you would see the glory of God?" So they took away the stone. Then Jesus looked up and said, "Father, I thank you that you have heard me. I knew that you always hear me, but I said this for the benefit of the people standing here, that they may believe that you sent me."

When he had said this, Jesus called in a loud voice, "Lazarus, come out!" The dead man came out, his hands and feet wrapped with strips of linen, and a cloth around his face. Jesus said to them, "Take off the grave clothes and let him go." (John 11:1-44).

Children of God I would love you to try as much as you can to soak the above scripture into your spirit and get the deep revelation. The bible declares that a time came that some people was sent to inform Jesus in another region that, the one that He love is sick so preferably he must come and heal him of his sickness. Believers after Jesus heard the news He didn't pay attention to the one that he claimed he love and never went to heal Lazarus and he died.

Brothers and sisters I would love you to put your self in Lazarus position, how would you feel if the one that you claim you love and He also loves you treat you in that manner, I believe you going to feel the same as Lazarus did, die in pains, broken hearted, hatred and you will even feel of separating from your friendship.

Believers this is very painful and it also gives us the wisdom that the one you love can at times hurt you also break your heart but please this shouldn't give you the platform or the opportunity to divorce or separate from your love one.

Please let see the wisdom, knowledge and deep revelation Jesus was trying to let us learn from what He did. Believers we realized that when Jesus never went to heal Lazarus, he died. And the people again brought the information to Jesus that the one He love is now dead. Jesus now gathered his disciples and went to where Lazarus was buried and the bible made it clear that He went and rose up Lazarus who was dead for four good days.

Children of God isn't this powerful, I know that healing some one is easier than raising some one from his or her death but Jesus our Lord and master saviour was trying to let us learn something deep and good from his actions. Brothers and sisters right from what the holy spirit has just reveal to us means that when we are hurt from our love one's or partners we shouldn't break up, divorce or separate but rather fix it no matter how wrong we are or difficult it is because Jesus went to fix His.

Now this is the powerful part of the story and with the supernatural gift God has deposited in us, which is our voice. Believers would you understand and also bare with me that Jesus went to raise Lazarus from death by using his voice.

> When he had said this, Jesus called in a loud **voice**, "Lazarus, come out!" The dead man came out, his hands and feet wrapped with strips of linen, and a cloth around his face.

> Jesus said to them, "Take off the grave clothes and let him go." (John 11:43-44).

Believers imagine if there were no voice to operate and manifest with, how would have this process be possible because anytime you need something alive or dead to hear you, you need your voice to bring your words out for hearing.

Precious one our voice is powerful and a supernatural gift indeed.

Based on this revelation from the Holy Spirit, I've now come to realize that many marriages have suffered and are still suffering from separation and divorce because the couples lack the concept of using their voices humbly toward each other. They don't show humility or talk to each other lovingly in their marriages, and it causes divorce or, at the least, separation.

Believers, when it comes to the subject of marriage, it's a very broad topic to analyze.

But the Holy Spirit draws to my attention that today many marriages suffer divorce and separation because both the man and the woman ignore the idea of talking to each other humbly, smoothly, nicely, and lovingly. I believe strongly that if you are a woman or a man who knows how to use your voice beautifully toward your partner; you will keep the love, togetherness, and happiness in you and your partner from everlasting to everlasting and you will live happily ever after.

As a young Christian, growing up, I witnessed so many marriages around me and at times saw couples fight over a little misunderstanding and instead of apologizing to one another allow the devil to take control and sit on their minds. They would not talk to each other for several days, which led them to seek happiness outside their marriages and right there and then you would find them separated.

But I tell you the truth, if you are a man or a woman and know how to talk to your husband or wife humbly with your beautiful voice, you will get the supernatural keys to open him or her up anytime you want your partner to manifest in a different direction, because there is much power in mankind's voice.

Believers, based on the revelations in this book, I urge you to use your *voice* humbly in your matrimonial homes. My brothers and sisters, all this time, the answer to bringing success to your marriage has been just to manifest it through your voice righteously and humbly toward your partner.

I hope we all know and believe so strongly that the man is the head of the family. In reality, it is true, but emotionally, it is the woman, because in most cases, what the man does in the family (home) is based on instruction from the wife, which she has given during the early hours before dawn comes. Because it is women who are most in the house and who spend a lot of time with the children, they know what goes in and comes out. So the woman gives a report to the husband and gives her solutions and advice as well in what should be done.

Therefore, if you are a woman who knows how to operate your voice humbly, you will gain favor in the sight of your husband, day in and day out.

This reminds me of a story at the beginning of the Bible in Genesis. Our grandfather Abraham was a very great man of God, a strong prophet of the Lord, but he was being manipulated by the sweet voice of his wife Sarah.

I hope we remember the story; there is a deep revelation behind it.

> Now Sarai, Abram's wife had borne him no children. But she had an Egyptian maidservant named Hagar; so she said to Abram, "The LORD has kept me from having children. Go, sleep with my maidservant; perhaps I can build a family through her." Abram agreed to what Sarah said. So after Abram had been living in Canaan ten years, Sarah his wife took her Egyptian maidservant Hagar and gave her to her husband to be his wife.

> He slept with Hagar, and she conceived. When she knew she was pregnant, she began to despise her mistress. Then Sarah said to Abram, "You are responsible for the wrong I am suffering. I put my servant in your arms, and now that she knows she is pregnant, she despises me. May the LORD judge between you and me?"

"Your servant is in your hands," Abram said. "Do with her whatever you think well." Then Sarah ill-treated Hagar; so she fled from her.

The angel of the LORD found Hagar near a spring in the desert; it was the spring that is beside the road to Shur. And he said, "Hagar, servant of Sarah, where are you going?"

"I'm running away from my mistress Sarai," she answered.

Then the angel of the LORD told her, "Go back to your mistress and submit to her." The angel added, "I will so increase your descendants that they will be too numerous to count." The angel of the LORD also said to her: "You are now with child and you will have a son. You shall name him Ishmael, for the LORD has heard of your misery. He will be a wild donkey of a man; his hand will be against everyone's hand against him, and he will live in hostility towards all his brothers."

She gave this name to the LORD who spoke to her: "You are the God who sees me," for she said, "I have now seen the one who sees me." That is why the well was called Beer LahaiRoi; it is still there, between Kadesh and Bered. So Hagar bore Abram a son, and Abram gave the name Ishmael to the son she had borne. Abram was eighty-six years old when Hagar bore him Ishmael. (Genesis 16:1-16)

We all could understand and notice from the above story how Sarah, Abraham's wife could convince Abraham to go to bed with her slave Hagar for her to give them a baby even though the Lord had prophesied onto their lives that they would have a baby by themselves.

After Hagar gave birth to Ishmael, Sarah convinced Abraham to drive the slave and the child away because she felt the slave (Hagar) hated her, which Abraham did by driving them away. But an angel from the Lord met Hagar and the baby on their way to a place of which they had no idea, and the Lord sent them back to Abraham's household again.

But after sometime, when Isaac was born, Sarah once again manipulated Abraham to drive Hagar and the child out of their sight, for she couldn't stand to see her son Isaac shares properties with Ishmael. This was very disturbing, because Ishmael was also Abraham's seed, but he listened to his wife. I need you to imagine what your voice can do to bring you success in anything you want to do in this life.

But, Believers, we all believe and know perfectly that our grandfather Abraham was a great man and a prophet of the Lord, who sought the face of the Lord Day in, day out. Going through the Bible, we even remember the promises the Lord made to him directly, but yet his dear wife can control him with her voice.

Believers, there is much power in your voice. Only if you will use it righteously and humbly you will succeed in all that you want to accomplish in this life.

And with a righteous and humble voice, you will hold and keep your marriage from everlasting to everlasting. Just imagine a very strong man of God who seeks the face of the Lord and who prophesies, and yet with her sweet, lovely, and humble voice of the wife could control him as if he were under an enchantment.

Believers, this gives you a deep revelation that with your voice, you can achieve success in all that you want to accomplish. And as Sarah our grandmother gained success in her marriage, so we can also gain success in our marriages. If only we use our voice lovingly and kindly toward our partners. Sarah never wanted to share her husband with another woman, and with her voice, she accomplished her wish, so as you can gain success, if you don't want to share your partner with anyone, you will not have to do so.

Lest I forget, this powerful voice, which holds so much influence in marriage, began during the time when Adam and Eve were created. As we already know the story, we remember how Eve convinced Adam with her powerful and sweet voice to eat the forbidden fruit, which the Lord had commanded and instructed them not to eat.

> Now the serpent was craftier than any of the wild animals the LORD God had made. He said to the woman, "Did God really say, 'You must not eat fruit from the tree in the garden'?"

> The woman said to the serpent, "We may eat from the trees in the garden, but God did say, 'You must not eat fruit from the tree that is in the middle of the garden, and you must not touch it, or you will die.'"

> "You will not surely die," the serpent said to the woman. "For God knows that when you eat of it your eyes will be opened and you will be like God knowing good and evil."

When the woman saw that the fruit of the tree was good for food and pleasing to the eye, and also desirable for gaining wisdom, she took some and ate it. She also gave some to her husband, who was with her, and he ate it.

Then the eyes of both of them opened, and they realized that they were naked; so they sewed fig leaves together and made coverings for themselves.

Then the man and his wife heard the sound of the LORD God as he was walking in the garden in the cool day, and they hid from the LORD God among the trees of the garden. But the LORD God called to the man, "Where are you?"

He answered, "I heard you in the garden, and I was afraid because I was naked; so I hid."

And he said, "Who told you that you were naked? Have you eaten from the tree from which I commanded you not to eat?"

The man said, "The woman you put here with me—she gave me some fruit from the tree, and I ate it."

Then the LORD God said to the woman, "What is this you have done?"

The woman said, "The serpent deceived me, and I ate."

So the LORD God said to the serpent, "Because you have done this, 'Cursed are you above all the livestock and all the animals! You will crawl on your belly and you will eat dust all the days of your life. And I will put enmity between your offspring and hers; he will crush your head, and you will strike his heel.'"

To the woman he said, "I will greatly increase your pains in child bearing; with pain you will give birth to children. Your desire will be for your husband, and he will rule over you."

To Adam he said, "Because you listened to your wife and ate from the tree about which I commanded you, 'You must not eat of it,' 'Cursed is the ground because of you; through painful toil you will eat of it all the days of your life. It will produce thorns and thistles for you and you will eat the plants of the field. By the sweat of your brow you will eat your food until you return to the ground, since from it you were taken; for dust you are and to dust you will return."

Adam named his wife Eve because she would become the mother of all the living.

The LORD God made garments of skin for Adam and his wife and clothed them. And the LORD God said, "The man has now become like one of us, knowing good and evil. He must not be allowed to reach out his hand and take also from the tree of life and eat, and live forever." So the LORD God banished him from the Garden of Eden to work the ground from which he had been taken. After he drove the man out, he placed on the east side of the Garden of Eden cherubim and a flaming sword flashing back and forth to guard the way to the tree of life. (Genesis 3:1-24)

Believers, isn't this supernatural voice we have so powerful? With your voice, you can achieve everything and anything you want to accomplish.

I urge you to use your voice righteously and humbly in your marriage from now on, and if you are ever at the point of losing your partner, remember it is not too late to use your sweet voice kindly to apologize, for there is much power in our voices.

My dear Christians, marriage is an honor to God. God honors marriage; he authorized it and established it after the creation of mankind in the Garden of Eden.

Believers, God honored marriage and instituted marriage to mankind.

> The LORD God said, "It is not good for the man to be alone. I will make a helper suitable for him." Now the LORD God had formed out of the ground all the beasts of the field and all the birds of the air. He brought them to the man to see what he would name them; and whatever the man called each living creature, that was its name. So the man gave names to all the livestock, the birds of the air and all the beasts of the field.

> But for Adam no suitable helper was found. So the LORD God caused the man to fall into a deep sleep; and while he

was sleeping, he took one of the man's ribs and closed up the place with flesh. Then the LORD God made a woman from the rib he had taken out of the man, and he brought her to the man.

The man said, "This is now bone of my bones and flesh of my flesh; she shall be called 'woman,' for she was taken out of man." For this reason a man will leave his father and mother and be united to his wife, and they will become one flesh. (Genesis 2:18-24)

Therefore, it is not good for mankind to rebel against the authority and honor God has instituted, for if anyone rebels against the authority that God has instituted, that means he or she is disobeying and rebelling against God and that person is causing or bringing judgment upon himself or herself.

God's purpose for marriage is to inspire mankind to happiness and everlasting joy.

"The LORD God said, 'It is not good for the man to be alone. I will make a helper suitable for him'" (Genesis 2:18).

In marriage, one is to express love intimately and may have children; because of this, God, who instituted marriage, does not find pleasure in separation and divorce. For what God has put together, let no one put asunder. Therefore, couples (both husband and wife) must treat each other with love and respect. Both husband and wife must be in submission to each other for permanency in their marriage, and there will be unity in their marriage for ever and ever.

Let me share with you a disturbing question bothering the Pharisees and came to ask Jesus during his ministry about divorce concerning marriage:

> Some Pharisees came to him to test him. They asked, "Is it lawful for a man to divorce his wife for any and every reason?"
>
> "Haven't you read," he replied, "That at the beginning the Creator 'made them male and female,' and said, 'For this reason a man will leave his father and mother and be united to his wife, and the two will become one flesh'? So they are no longer two, but one. Therefore what God has joined together, let man not separate. . . . I tell you that anyone who divorces his wife, except for marital unfaithfulness, and marries another woman commits adultery." (Matthew 19:3-6, 9)

There must also be equal responsibility between both partners. At this point, I would like to cast your mind back to our grandparents Abraham and Sarah, how they had a lifelong and sweet marriage, because they respected each other and expressed love intimately toward each other. Even Sarah who was said to be Abraham's wife called her husband, "Master."

This shows you how respectful Sarah was, and there was nothing that Sarah requested from Abraham that he refused to grant. Because she had a voice and a sweet voice, of course, she used it righteously and humbly.

My fellow believers, at this moment, I hope you will believe with me that if you know how to talk to your partner, you will never suffer separation and divorce in your marriage. For God hates divorce, and divorce allows hardness of the heart, which will prevent you from serving God totally.

Believers, I recommend that you tune your voice toward your partner lovingly, sweetly, nicely, and wonderfully, for it is the voice that does everything under the sun. Your wife needs to be honored; she needs to be respected. Stop talking to her harshly (in an ugly way), and you will win her love, intimacy, and loyalty for life. Likewise, your husband needs to be honored; he needs to be respected. Talk to him lovingly and humbly, and he will be comforted anytime he sees his dear wife. And he will rush to come home after work because he knows his wife's voice is as sweet as honey and will comfort him to pull through his hard day's work.

Even Isaac, our father, was much disturbed and very unhappy after his mother Sarah died, but the Bible declared that as soon as Isaac saw Rebecca, his wife, he was comforted.

> Isaac brought her into the tent of his mother Sarah and he married Rebekah. So she became his wife, and he loved her; and Isaac was comforted after his mother's death. (Genesis 24:67)

Believers, marriage is a beautiful thing; that's why God instituted it. Therefore, treat your partner with humbleness, and the union in your marriage will last forever.

I remember when I was young, I heard a story about this couple (a husband and wife) who had a quarrel. After the quarrel, their hearts were filled with the spirit of pride, but no humbleness, so the devil took advantage of their weakness and came to sit on their minds, which made them refuse to apologize to each other.

But they still lived together, though they refused to talk to each other; funnily enough, they communicated through writing notes to each another. After some weeks, the man got a contract from a very big and famous company, which was worth millions.

Now with this, the man wrote a note to his wife when he came home that evening concerning his contract, but the issue was he would need to wake up early, like 6:00 a.m. the next morning, to go for an interview with the new company he had gotten a contract with; so in the note, he told the wife to wake him up the next morning.

Since they were not speaking with their voices, the next morning, when it was 6:00 a.m., the woman also wrote a note and left it beside the husband saying, "It is 6:00 a.m., so wake up to go for your interview." What a tragedy, the man woke up at like 9:00 a.m. in the morning and saw the letter beside him.

Oops! He began to cry, and he cried very hard because the time for his interview had passed. He had lost his multimillion-dollar contract. Believers, this led to their divorce (separation).

I hope you can imagine a situation like this. It is a very bad habit; just see how some couples who refuse to use their voices have ended their marriages. They lose both money (multimillions in the previous example) and their precious marriage. My fellow Christians, I hope you know very well that "what God has put together let no man put asunder."

Believers, Jesus made us understand in the Bible that you can only divorce your wife based on marital unfaithfulness, and even with that, if you think you still love her, you can make amends with her and still go on with your marriage.

After reading this book, I would love for you to use and manifest your voice to operate in your marriage no matter how difficult it is, for there are greater powers in our voice.

Even Delilah, who was said in the Bible to be Samson's downfall, didn't use just a day to convince Samson but kept on trying until she succeeded. I hope you remember that story:

> One day Samson went to Gaza, where he saw a prostitute. He went in to spend the night with her. The people of Gaza were told, "Samson is here!" So they surrounded the place and lay in wait for him all night at the city gate. They made no move during the night, saying, "At dawn we'll kill him." But Samson lay there only until the middle of the night.
>
> Then he got up and took hold of the doors of the city gate, together with the two posts, and tore them loose, bar and all. He lifted them to his shoulders and carried them to the top of the hill that faces Hebron. Sometime later, he fell in love with a woman in the Valley of Sorek whose name was Delilah.
>
> The rulers of the Philistines went to her and said, "See if you can lure him into showing you the secret of his great strength and how we can overpower him so that we may

tie him up and subdue him. Each one of us will give you eleven hundred shekels of silver."

So Delilah said to Samson, "Tell me the secret of your great strength and how you can be tied up and subdued."

Samson answered her, "If anyone ties me with seven fresh thongs that have not been dried, I'll become as weak as any other man."

Then the rulers of the Philistines brought her seven fresh thongs that had not been dried, and she tied him with them. With men hidden in the room, she called to him, "Samson, the Philistines are upon you!" But he snapped the thongs as easily as a piece of string snaps when it comes close to a flame.

So the secret of his strength was not discovered. Then Delilah said to Samson, "You have made a fool of me; you lied to me. Come now, tell me how you can be tied."

He said, "If anyone ties me securely with new ropes that have never been used, I'll become as weak as any other man."

So Delilah took new ropes and tied him with them. Then, with men hidden in the room, she called to him, "Samson, the Philistines are upon you!" But he snapped the ropes off his arms as if they were threads. Delilah then said to Samson, "Until now, you have been making a fool of me and lying to me. Tell me how you can be tied."

He replied, "If you weave the seven braids of my head into the fabric on the loom and tighten it with the pin, I'll become as weak as any other man." So while he was sleeping, Delilah took the seven braids of his head, wove them into the fabric and tightened it with the pin.

Again she called to him, "Samson, the Philistines are upon you!" He awoke from his sleep and pulled up the pin and the loom, with the fabric. Then she said to him, "How can you say, 'I love you,' when you won't confide in me? This is the third time you have made a fool of me and haven't told me the secret of your great strength." With such nagging she prodded him day after day until he was tired to death.

So he told her everything. "No razor has ever been used on my head," he said, "because I have been a Nazirite set apart to God since birth. If my head were shaved, my strength would leave me, and I would become as weak as any other man."

When Delilah saw that he had told her everything, she sent word to the rulers of the Philistines, "Come back once more; he has told me everything." So the rulers of the Philistines returned with the silver in their hands.

Having put him to sleep on her lap, she called a man to shave off the seven braids of his hair, and so began to subdue him. And his strength left him. Then she called, "Samson, the Philistines are upon you!"

He awoke from his sleep and thought, "I'll go out as before and shake myself free." But he did not know that the LORD had left him. Then the Philistines seized him, gouged out his eyes, and took him down to Gaza. Binding him with bronze shackles, they set him to grinding in the prison.

But the hair on his head began to grow again after it had been shaved. (Judges 16:1-22)

Believers, the deep revelations in this book will challenge you to use your voice humbly toward your partner. You will then succeed in your marriage.

Chapter Six

Prosperity, Riches, and Fame

A gift opens the way for the giver and ushers him into the presence of the great.

(Proverbs 18:16)

$\mathcal{M}$ Y FELLOW BELIEVERS, I hope you will also agree with me at this point that it is our voice that make us *rich*, *famous*, and *prosperous*. Believers, I need all of you to think about all the superstars, celebrities, great men and women of God around you, whom you see or hear on the radio, television, or Internet and in magazines and newspapers. You will find that they are all blessed, successful, rich, and famous today because of one thing: their *voices*.

With voices, musicians have been singing, great men of God have been preaching, and superstars and celebrities have been doing shows and interviews and also going for tours and organizing programs to the four corners of the Earth.

Just imagine if there were no voices, who would have been famous, rich, and successful? And with these superstars, celebrities, and great people of God, if they had no voices, how would people listen to them, how would they have become rich, and what would they even be rich of?

Brothers and Sisters, I proclaim to you that without voice, there would be no activity that would go on under the sun, but even if there should be activities, the world wouldn't be as interesting as it is now.

Beloved, I know you're thinking, but you still need to think harder and imagine how voice makes a great impact in God's creation (the universe).

Believers, have you ever noticed that your voice makes these musicians, superstars, celebrities, and great people around you, whoever they are? Why? Because if a person invents or discovers something great in the world and no one talks about it, people don't praise this person; nobody recommends him or her. This person will never be great because no one is giving him or her recognition, no one is elevating him or her, and no one is praising him or her for people to know that whatever he or she has done is great.

Suppose a musician comes out with a new song, and people don't mention or talk about this song, and even his or her fans don't speak of it, trying to let people know that the new song is a hit; the beloved musician will never be uplifted because people are not using their voices to praise him or her.

Now I need you to accept the fact that it is your voice that makes the musicians, superstars, and celebrities great, honored, rich, and famous.

My dear people, I hope you get the picture. It is your praising voice that makes people great, because you make comments—good comments of course—so that people will acknowledge them. So, my precious people, my question is: why are you praising people with your voice so they will be rich and continue to be great while you sit down and remain nothing, instead of also inventing or innovating something for which people will praise you and talk about you so that you can also be rich and famous? Ask yourself why you are always praising these stars and celebrities, but you don't get their attention to praise you? It is because you can recognize their voice, but they don't recognize yours; you can identify their voice but they can't identify yours.

In fact, it is very sad that we can recognize people's voices even when we haven't seen them but have heard them on the radio; we can identify them and be happy for them because they are being blessed. But have you asked yourself, do they even know you? Or will they be happy for you if they see you sitting home and doing nothing with your life? I urge you, Children of God, everybody in this world has a talent; therefore be happy that you are not deaf mute and dumb, and you can also do something so people can hear you or see you.

This pushes me to remember when Jesus began his ministry on earth. Many rich, famous, and great people invited him to come into their houses to spend time, enjoy, and be happy. This is because Jesus's voice made him a superstar or a celebrity.

I hope we can remember the scriptures that tell of the woman who anointed the feet of Jesus with the most expensive and outrageous perfume. (It was even said in the scriptures that the perfume would better have been sold and the proceeds given to the poor.)

This tells us how extraordinary the perfume was, let read it from the Holy Scripture:

> While Jesus was in Bethany in the home of a man known as Simon the Leper, a woman came to him with an alabaster jar of very expensive perfume, which she poured on his head as he was reclining at the table.
>
> When the disciples saw this, they were indignant. "Why this waste?" they asked. "This perfume could have been sold at a high price and the money given to the poor."
>
> Aware of this, Jesus said to them, "Why are you bothering this woman? She has done a beautiful thing to me. The poor you will always have with you, but you will not always have me. When she poured this perfume on my body, she did it to prepare me for burial. I tell you the truth, wherever this gospel is preached throughout the world, what she has done will also be told in memory of her." (Matthew 26:6-13)

In the above story, we notice the woman with the perfume is feeling different from how she used to feel before. The voice of Jesus has pierced her heart, and salvation has been imparted unto her beloved this is powerful and very hard to understand if the Holy Spirit does not enlight certains things to you but I pray you will totally understand after reading.

Lets also look at a story about a tax collector;

A certain man called Zacchaeus was said to be a tax collector—in fact, the description of this man in the Bible makes us aware of his great riches and fame. But this man had heard of Jesus Christ, and his wish was to hear him speak.

The Bible tells an interesting story about this man—how the voice of Jesus Christ could get this *great, rich,* and *famous* man to climb a tree to witness Jesus Christ speaking (preaching).

> *Jesus entered Jericho and was passing through. A man was there by the name of Zacchaeus; he was a chief tax collector and was wealthy. He wanted to see who Jesus was, but being a short man he could not, because of the crowd. So he ran ahead and climbed a sycamore-fig tree to see him, since Jesus was coming that way. When Jesus reached the spot, he looked up and said to him, "Zacchaeus, come down immediately. I must stay at your house today." So he came down at once and welcomed him gladly.*
>
> *All the people saw this and began to mutter, "He has gone to be the guest of a 'sinner.'"*
>
> *But Zacchaeus stood up and said to the Lord, "Look, Lord! Here and now I give half of my possessions to the poor, and if I have cheated anybody out of anything, I will payback four times the amount."* (Luke 19:1-8)

Isn't the above story very interesting? The powerful voice of Jesus Christ brought him fame; many rich and great people were running after him.

This is quite marvelous; people of dignity are trying to do whatever possible to hear and listen to the voice of Jesus Christ. Just imagine, your voice is making people of great wealth climb trees to hear you and travel back and forth to listen to what you have to say because they feel great power in your voice. That's why at times you will see shows with preaching and the auditorium will be full of presidents, celebrities, and ministers, men and women of God, because of what they have to say or do with their *voice*.

Believers, during the time of Jesus Christ on earth, his voice made him stand before kings, rich and great people in that era. Even during the time of his crucifixion, all the kings from different regions in that city wanted to hear him, because of his proclamation of being the son of God.

I even remember how a very great and rich man, who was a good teacher of the Law of Moses, would sneak out of the temple and come to Jesus at night to hear him and learn more because he realized that there was much power in the voice of Jesus Christ.

The Bible described this man as a very great, rich, and famous scholar of the Law of Moses.

> Now there was a man of the Pharisees named Nicodemus, a member of the Jewish ruling council. He came to Jesus at night and said, "Rabbi, we know you are a teacher who has come from God. For no-one could perform the miraculous signs you are doing if God were not with him."

In reply Jesus declared, "I tell you the truth, no-one can see the kingdom of God unless he is born again."

"How can a man be born when he is old?" Nicodemus asked. "Surely he cannot enter a second time into his mother's womb to be born!"

Jesus answered, "I tell you the truth, no-one can enter the Kingdom of God unless he is born of water and the Spirit. Flesh gives birth to flesh, but the spirit gives birth to spirit. You should not be surprised at my saying, 'You must be born again.' The wind blows wherever it pleases. You hear its sound, but you cannot tell where it comes from or where it is going. So it is with everyone born of the Spirit."

"How can this be?" Nicodemus asked.

"You are Israel's teacher," said Jesus, "and do you not understand these things? I tell you the truth, we speak of what we know, and we testify to what we have seen, but still you people do not accept our testimony. I have spoken to you of earthly things and you do not believe; how then will you believe if I speak heavenly things?" (John 3:1-12)

Beloved, the question is why should this man come to Jesus at night but not during the day, and he even came secretly. From whom was he hiding? Was it his colleagues or the audience, members who knew of his position in the city or at the temple? I believe he was too rich and famous to come to Jesus, instead of having Jesus come to him.

Now this man, rich and famous in the town was after Jesus Christ. He was very eager to hear more of Jesus's voice, because he realized there was so much *power* in the voice of Jesus. He speaks and it brings forth something. Believers, this is very incredible, but why? Because the voice of Jesus made people of great riches and the famous and successful run after him. Isn't this supernatural, that's by your voice, riches and fame can run after you?

Have you ever noticed or has it ever come to your mind that the devil (Satan) does not manufacture money? The devil does not produce or make money; his powers and everything he has was given to him by God. So don't you think that all the riches and blessings in the world are the Lord's?

Therefore, whoever is blessed in the world is from God; all the rich and famous people in the world were caused to be blessed by the Lord.

The Bible made it clear that money—gold, silver, and riches—are for the Lord; therefore, if the Lord does not cause you to be rich or successful in this life, you will never be blessed.

Believers, the Bible has also made it clear that:

"The earth is of the Lord and everything in it, the world, and all who live in it" (Psalm 24:1).

So, People of God, it is the Lord who makes someone rich and also poor, and unless the Lord grants you success, you can never be successful. And the Lord, being so good, does not show favoritism when it comes to his creation. He has deposited in mankind one thing that can make us successful in life, which is a supernatural talent everyone under the sun has.

Believers, God has given to mankind talents, which I believe so strongly that all men and women have. People of God, think about this again: what gift or talents which exist under the sun that you will never need your *voice* to operate?

Imagine if the president in your country had no voice to talk, convince, and command; who would have voted for him or her to come to power?

At this point, I pray and believe something has been dropped into your system that makes you believe and totally comprehend that it is the "power of voice" that fulfills or accomplishes mankind's success in everything in this life.

Jesus once made a statement in the scriptures that *"I tel you the truth, the tax collectors and the prostitutes (pagans) are entering the kingdom of God ahead of you.* (Matthew 21:31)

Who are the pagans, Believers? The pagans are the people we Christians believe to be unbelievers.

Therefore, if these people are going to the kingdom of God, Believers, then it is likely that they are also being blessed, gaining riches and fame ahead of us (Christians). Why should Jesus make such a statement? Is it because they are doing something extraordinary we don't know about, as Christians, or do they serve God secretly? I guess not!

But what I will say to this is, may be we Christians love passing judgment on unbelievers, and in doing that, we lose focus on our own way, especially musicians who do not make songs that testify about God.

Believers often talk a lot against their music, but yet these people are still gaining riches and fame and enjoying luxurious lives. Believers, this is not to support certain types of gains; I mean they are manifesting their talents by operating with their voices. Who gave them their voices? Wasn't it God? So why don't you also righteously manifest and operate in your talents, rather than waiting for these unbelievers to get wealth, riches, and fame ahead of you?

Jesus once told a parable to his disciples about God-given talents:

> Again, it will be like a man going on a journey, which called his servants and entrusted his property to them. To one he gave five talents of money, to another two talents, and to another one talent, each according to his ability. Then he went on his journey.

> The man who had received the five talents went at once and put his money to work and gained five more. So also, the one with the two talents gained two more. But the man who had received one talent went off, dug a hole in the ground and hid his master's money.

> After a long time the master of those servants returned and settled accounts with them. The man who had received the five talents brought the other five. "Master," he said, "you entrusted me with five talents. See, I have gained five more."

His master replied, "Well done, good and faithful servant! You have been faithful with a few things; I will put you in charge of many things. Come and share your master's happiness!"

The man with two talents also came. "Master," he said, "you entrusted me with two talents; see, I have gained two more."

His master replied, "Well done, good and faithful servant! You have been faithful with a few things; I will put you in charge of many things. Come and share your master's happiness!"

Then the man who had received the one talent came. "Master," he said, "I knew that you are a hard man, harvesting where you have not sown and gathering where you have not scattered seed. So I was afraid and went out and hid your talent in the ground. See, here is what belongs to you."

His master replied, "You wicked, lazy servant! So you knew that I harvested where I have not sown and gather where I have not scattered seed? Well then, you should have put my money on deposit with the bankers, so that when I returned I would have received it back with interest. Take the talent from him and give it to the one who has the ten talents. For everyone who has will be given more, and they will have abundance. Whoever does not have, even what he has will be taken from him. And throw that worthless servant outside, into the darkness, where there will be weeping and gnashing of teeth." (Matthew 25:14-30)

Children of God, the above story is very fascinating. You can understand very clearly that if you aren't fruitful with the gifts or talents the Lord has blessed you with, it is going to lead to your eternal destruction.

This made me get the revelation that what is needed for us to get to heaven might not be just living a righteous life, gaining good deeds or seeking after knowledge but also can be based on the assignment God has entrusted to us. For in life I believe that if you don't have a purpose at your destination you will never get there. Therefore children of God do you think if we have no purpose on this earth God would have brought us here, I tell you we do; does why we are here so we must manifest to continue the Lords creation.

Believers, this again reminds me of a story in the Bible. Jesus Christ was once walking with his disciples and after preaching and evangelizing came to a certain place. He was very hungry and walked up to a tree. Very unfortunately for the tree, it had no fruit, and Jesus cursed the tree to perish. The tree immediately decayed.

> Early in the morning, as he was on his way back to the city, he was very hungry. Seeing a fig tree by the road, he went up to it but found nothing on it except leaves. Then he said to it, "May you never bear fruit again." Immediately the tree withered. (Matthew 21:18-19)

My dear Christians, imagine if you were Jesus at that hungry moment; what would you do? You would have commanded the same tree to bear fruit and eaten of it. But Jesus cursed the tree; the reason is not that Jesus Christ couldn't cause the tree to bear fruit but that he wanted mankind to learn something from that miracle.

This means that for any living thing that needs to bear fruit with your talents or gifts and you refuse to do so, Jesus is going to curse you at the appropriate time when he walks up to you and finds out that you have not borne any fruit.

At this point I know one will be bothered with the question, what about our brothers and sisters out there who are disabling how they can be successful. But I challenge you with the deep revelation from this book that they only need their voice to reposition thierselves, because until you are mute deaf and dump you can be what ever you want to become in this life therefore I have seen or heard the blind, cripple, maimed, lame and amputated become a superstar, celebrity, rich, famous and successful in th world.

The ones we don't see or hear them progressing are those who are timid to do something with their voice because of their situation. Precious one I believe you have been touched by the supernatural gift from God, which is your voice. You might be a disable reading this book but I challenge you that after reading this book be encourage to make a move and you will be a survival, try to do something with your voice and the world will hear you.

I pray you enjoy, stay blessed.

Chapter Seven

Satan's Powerful Tool (*Voice*)

*B*ELIEVERS, THIS CHAPTER reveals the effectiveness, the power, the blessings, and the benefits of our voice as a supernatural gift from God.

You know, children of God believe so strongly that the devil is one of the most powerful, beautiful, charming, and lovely angels from heaven; yes, this is true, but what specifically was he known for, apart from all these features?

If he is as powerful as we think he is, why did it take only Archangel Michael and his army commanders to defeat the devil when war broke out in heaven?

"And there was a war in heaven. Michael and his angels fought against the dragon, and the dragon and his angels fought back" (Revelation 12:7).

Believers, the devil is not as powerful as we think he is, but through the deep revelation knowledge from the Holy Spirit, we know he has a powerful voice and his voice has been his most powerful tool forever. This is the strategy he uses to destroy mankind.

Therefore, the only way for mankind to fight back is also to use our powerful voice to pray against him and bring him to divine judgment. God has given mankind authority and dominion; our voice is the greatest tool to resist and overcome Lucifer when we use it to condemn him through prayer.

In fact, God has given us a voice, and we need to let the devil identify and recognize us and know where we stand in the name of our Lord and master, our savior Jesus Christ.

Have you ever thought of the devil, that he is just an ordinary angel? Yes, the devil was an angel in heaven, and angels were created to worship, praise, and serve God and to be God's messengers. So think about this, the devil (Lucifer) had the characteristics, features, duties, and responsibilities of an angel.

So as an angel, he did not have any extraordinary powers; the only gift he was highly anointed in was his *voice*, which he was to use:

❖ To sing

❖ To worship

❖ To praise

❖ To lead a group of angels when it came to singing, praising, and worshipping the highest God.

The Bible makes us understand that he was a leader of the singers. The only position the devil had was as a leader of the angels who worship, praise, and sing for God.

And come to think of it, each and every single angel in heaven has his or her own position, duties, and responsibilities. Angels do not all have the same positions and powers.

Some angels were created to fight. Others are great messengers of God. Some are very close to the throne of grace, which means they are very close to God.

Examples include:

- Archangel Michael—commander of the group of angels in heaven who fight battles

- Angel Gabriel—a great angel and a messenger of God

- Seraph—a powerful angel, very close to God; they have six wings and are full of fire; they could help clean or take away mankind's sins (Isaiah 6:6-7)

- Cherubim—powerful angels, very close to God; they have six wings and are full of fire.

There are also some highly anointed and powerful spirits, creatures, and elders whom God made to be close to him in heaven. They are very powerful and highly anointed in wisdom and knowledge, even more than angels. They include:

1. Four living creatures

2. Twenty-four elders

3. Seven spirits of God

So think about this: the devil, as an angel, is not as powerful as the angels, elders, spirits, and creatures I have talked about or listed above. He (Satan) was just an angel, an angel gifted and anointed with a *voice* to sing, praise, and worship God. And come to think of it, his voice was very sweet, interesting, and lovely. When he sang, he moved God.

> How you have fallen from heaven, O morning star, son of the dawn! You have been cast down to the earth, you who once laid low the nations!
>
> You said in your heart, "I will ascend to heaven; I will raise my throne above the stars of God; I will sit enthroned on the mount of assembly, on the utmost heights of the sacred mountain. I will ascend above the tops of the clouds; I will make myself like the most high." But you are brought down to the grave, to the depths of the pit. (Isaiah 14:12-15)

From the above passage, we get the picture of what Lucifer was thinking and saying. And that is why he was overwhelmed by pride and sinned against God. He realized that he could sing to move

God and thought, *When I sing, he becomes so happy, filled with joy; why then is all the praise and worship going to him and not me?*

And from this point, Lucifer became corrupted, and because of his sweet and lovely voice, he was able to convince, seduce, and deceive other angels into joining him in a war against God.

"And there was a war in heaven. Michael and his angels fought against the dragon, and the dragon and his angels fought back." (Revelation 12:7)

And that is why in the Garden of Eden he was able to convince, seduce, and deceive Adam's wife Eve to do what God had commanded them not to do, warned them against, and forbidden.

"Then the eyes of both of them were opened, and they realized that they were naked; so they sewed fig leaves together and made coverings for themselves" (Genesis 3:7).

Believers, reading the Bible and conducting revelation research, I realized the devil (Satan) never used force or pressure to lead people into negative acts (sin).

But what he does is use his powerful voice to gain control over you and use you to do his will. The Bible makes it clear that he (Satan) will steal, kill, and destroy.

Believers, the devil can never destroy you until he kills you, and he can never kill you until he steals you. Ask yourself why he can't kill and destroy you right away unless he steals you. The answer is that you are not his in the first place, and the only way to have you is to steal you first. Therefore, he only needs to use his powerful voice to steal you, so he can then have control and send you to destruction.

Let's look back in the scriptures, from the beginning of the Bible, in Genesis, after the creation of man and woman (Adam and Eve). The devil, known to be the old serpent, visited Eve, and with a sweet, lovely, and charming voice, convinced her to eat from a tree from which God had forbidden them to eat.

Now, when Eve ate the fruit, she also convinced Adam to eat from the same tree and that broke the loyalty between God and mankind.

Believers, I need you to picture something here: when the devil stole mankind to eat the forbidden fruit, it led mankind to destruction. God drove mankind away from his presence; therefore, believers, destruction would have never happened to mankind if the devil had not stolen Adam and Eve.

> Now the serpent was craftier than any of the wild animals the LORD God had made. He said to the woman, "Did God really say, 'You must not eat from any tree in the garden'?"

> The woman said to the serpent, "We may eat fruit from the trees in the garden, but God did say, 'You must not eat fruit from the tree that is in the middle of the garden, and you must not touch it, or you will die.'"

"You will not surely die," the serpent said to the woman. "For God knows that when you eat of it, your eyes will be like God, knowing good and evil."

When the woman saw that the fruit of the tree was good for food and pleasing to the eye, and also desirable for gaining wisdom, she took some and ate it. She also gave some to her husband, who was with her, and he ate it. Then the eyes of both of them were open, and they realized they were naked; so they sewed fig leaves together and made covering for themselves.

Then he and his wife heard the sound of the LORD God as he was walking in the garden in the cool of the day, and they hid from the LORD God among the trees of the garden. But the LORD God called to the man, "Where are you?"

He answered, "I heard you in the garden, and I was afraid because I was naked; so I hid."

And he said, "Who told you that you were naked? Have you eaten from the tree that I command you not to eat from?"

The man said, "The woman you put here with me—she gave me some fruit from the tree, and I ate it."

Then the LORD God said to the woman, "What is this you have done?"

The woman said, "The serpent deceived me and I ate it."

So the Lord God said to the serpent, "Because you have done this, cursed are you above all the livestock and all the wild animals! You will crawl on your belly and you will eat dust all the days of your life. And I will put enmity between you and the woman and between your offspring and hers; he will crush your head and you will strike his heel."

To the woman he said, "I will greatly increase your pains in childbearing; with pain you will give birth to children. Your desire will be for your husband and your husband will rule over you."

To Adam he said, "Because you listened to your wife and ate from the tree about which I command you, you must not eat of it, cursed is the ground because of you; through painful toil you will eat of it all the days of your life. It will produce thorns and thistles for you and you will eat the plants of the field. By the sweat of your brow you will eat your food until you return to the ground since from it you were taken; for dust you are and to dust you will return."

Adam named his wife Eve, because she would become the mother of all the living.

The LORD God made garments of skin for Adam and his wife and clothed them. And the LORD God said, "The man has become one of us, knowing good and evil. He must not be allowed to reach out his hand and take also from the tree of life and eat, and live forever."

So the LORD God banished him from the Garden of Eden to work the ground from which he had been taken. After he drove the man out, he placed on the east side of the Garden of Eden cherubim and a flaming sword flashing back and forth to guard the way to the tree of life. (Genesis 3:1-24)

Just see what the voice of the devil (Satan) can do if you are not strong enough. This tells us there is much power in our voice. Satan didn't use pressure and never forced mankind by any means; his voice was enough to steal, kill, and destroy.

My fellow Christians, I can stand strong on this revelation knowledge of the Holy Spirit that there is much power in our voice; therefore, it is about time we started using it to overcome our weaknesses and to gain fame, riches, and prosperity. We need to use our voice to stand for the Lord by preaching, praying, prophesying, and evangelizing.

Glory is to God, Believers, that Jesus Christ on earth also used the power of his voice to resist and fight against the devil, when Satan wanted to distract Jesus Christ from his mission on earth.

With the revelation knowledge from the Holy Spirit, I hope we can remember the temptation of Jesus Christ. During the life of Jesus Christ on earth, literally before he began his ministry, he fasted for forty days and nights after the spirit of the Lord led him into the desert, and there the devil showed himself to tempt him.

Then Jesus was led by the spirit into the desert to be tempted by the devil. After fasting for forty days and forty nights, he was hungry.

The tempter came to him and said, "If you are the Son of God, tell these stones to become bread."

Jesus answered, "It is written: 'Man does not live on bread alone, but on every word that comes from the mouth of God.'"

Then the devil took him to the holy city and had him stand on the highest point of the temple. "If you are the Son of God," he said, "throw yourself down. For it is written: 'He will command his angels concerning you, and they will lift you up in their hands, so that you will not strike your foot against a stone.'"

Jesus answered him, "It is also written: 'Do not put the Lord your God to the test.'"

Again, the devil took him to a very high mountain and showed him all the kingdoms of the world and their splendor. "All this I will give you," he said, "if you will bow down and worship me."

Jesus said to him, "Away from me, Satan! For it is written: 'Worship the Lord your God, and serve him only.'" Then the devil left him, and angels came and attended him. (Matthew 4:1-11)

Believers, just imagine how convincing, charming, sweet, and lovely the devil was in trying as hard as he could to lead Jesus Christ, the son of the living God, to destruction. But how awesome God is, that his son; Jesus, has a more powerful voice than the devil to pray against him, resist him, and overcome him (Satan).

People of God, I really want you to believe in and cherish the supernatural God-given gift that's your voice. Come out of yourself, and be blessed with your talents.

Why am I even accepting the fact that the voice is supernatural, People of God? Please think deeply on this revelation knowledge; it is something that cannot be seen but can be described; something that cannot be touched yet can be identified.

Isn't this mind-blowing, People of God? If you have good words but an ugly voice, you will be unknown, and even if you have ugly words but a sweet voice, people might take you as a comedian, which can make you famous.

Believers, your voice is the key and access to success in everything you are and will be in this journey of life.

Therefore, it is about time you rise and shine . . . ! Stay blessed.

A Short Prayer

May another level of revelatory knowledge of the anointing be released onto you as you read this book and the divine revelation power be deposited in your system.

May you be inspired by the Holy Spirit and be charged to do something with your voice after reading this book.

God bless you.

About the Author

Born in Ghana, West Africa, on the fifth day of the month of October, Emmanuel Bempong has learned to be spiritually strong and independent from the age of seventeen and has dedicated his life to doing the work of God.

Emmanuel Bempong is an entrepreneur; he is the CEO and president of the E-Save Group of Companies, E-Save Travel and Tours Inc., E-Save Productions and also runs a nongovernmental organization (NGO)—a charity organization that serves as an intermediary, taking donations from all over the world for orphans in Ghana, West Africa.

Emmanuel Bempong is an international evangelist with an uncompromising message of the salvation, the inspiration, and the powerful revelation that come from knowledge of God.

Being an international evangelist, Emmanuel Bempong has traveled to the United States of America, the United Kingdom, and other parts of the world because of his passion and love for the things of God.

Look for deeper revelatory knowledge books from Evangelist Emmanuel Bempong coming in the future.